BUSINESS BUILDERS
IN SWEETS AND TREATS

Young or old, just about everybody loves sweets and treats. Here, two young boys spend their money at a candy counter.

BUSINESS ☒ BUILDERS
IN SWEETS AND TREATS

Nathan Aaseng

The Oliver Press, Inc.
Minneapolis

The Oliver Press, Inc.
Charlotte Square
5707 West 36th Street
Minneapolis, MN 55416-2510

Library of Congress Cataloging-in-Publication Data
Aaseng, Nathan.
Business builders in sweets and treats / Nathan Aaseng
p. cm. — (Business builders ; 9)
Includes bibliographical references and index.
Contents: Milton Hershey: dreams made of chocolate — William Wrigley Jr.: Chicago's
chewing-gum empire — Frank and Forrest Mars: first family of candy — Vernon Rudolph:
Krispy Kreme Doughnuts: hottest brand going — Ellen Gordon: Tootsie Roll: making millions
on penny candy — Wally Amos: the cookie manager — Ben Cohen and Jerry Greenfield: good
will, good times, good ice cream.

1-881508-84-6 (library binding)
1. Candy industry—Biography—Juvenile literature. 2. Pastry industry—Biography—Juvenile
literature. 3. Businesspeople—United States—Biography—Juvenile literature. [1. Food industry and trade. 2. Businesspeople.] I. Title. II. Series.

HD9330.C652A26 2004
338.7'66415'0922—dc22
                                  2003064984

ISBN 1-881508-84-6
Printed in the United States of America

11 10 09 08 07 06 05   8 7 6 5 4 3 2 1

CONTENTS

Grow more
SUGAR BEETS
in 1945

MEET WARTIME
NEED FOR SUGAR

INTRODUCTION

SATISFYING
THE SWEET TOOTH

It is the main ingredient in food products that no one needs, yet many crave. Nearly 90 percent of the people who purchase items made from this substance do so on the spur of the moment. It is a food that contains no vital nutrients, but almost from the moment we are born, we have a strong desire for it in our diet.

Although it is a natural resource of no strategic military or technological importance, it has spurred historic advances in cross-cultural trade, prompted wars and diplomatic maneuvering. It has formed the backbone of the economy for a large portion of the subtropical and tropical Americas, and once stood at the center of a cruel system of slavery. The substance is sugar.

During World War II, quick-energy sweets were included in the rations given to soldiers. This poster encourages farmers to produce more sugar for those fighting overseas.

7

From earliest times, humans have wanted some form of concentrated sweetness in their diet. Written references to the first known sweetener, honey obtained from bees, are found in records from Central Asia dating back to 3000 B.C. The use of sweeteners most likely goes back even further than that, however—there are cave paintings in Spain that depict men stealing honey from honeycombs. These paintings are well over 8,000 years old!

At around this same time, inhabitants of the South Pacific land of New Guinea began cultivating sugar cane, a tall-growing species of grass that they had discovered contained a large amount of sweet-tasting material. Over time, they developed ways of extracting and purifying this material, which modern science calls sucrose and we know simply as sugar. Gradually, the techniques for growing and harvesting sugar cane spread to other Pacific and tropical regions.

"A REED WHICH MAKES HONEY WITHOUT BEES"

One of the first Westerners to come in contact with sugar cane was Alexander the Great, who first tasted it while on a military expedition from Greece to India in the fourth century B.C. One of his admirals wrote with amazement of "a reed which makes honey without bees." Nonetheless, it was not until the eleventh century that the use of cane sugar spread westward through Persia and into Europe. Sugar cane, which grew best in hot, humid climates, did not thrive in Europe, and throughout medieval times, it could be obtained only through the occasional

The word *sugar* most likely comes from *sarkar*, the Sanskrit word for grain. The Arabs translated this as *al zucar*, which became *azucar* in Spanish, *sucre* in French, *Zucker* in German, and, eventually, *sugar* in English.

Sucrose is only one of the many different types of sugar. Others include fructose, the sweetest natural sugar, which is found in fruit, vegetables, and honey; glucose (or dextrose), a sugar found in corn and honey; and maltose, a sugar made from grain called barley. Sugar alcohols like xylitol, mannitol, and sorbitol are absorbed differently by the body and are often used in "sugar free" products.

trade between East and West. It was a scarce and highly expensive luxury that only the wealthy could afford.

When Europeans came to the Americas in the late fifteenth century, however, the situation changed dramatically. Many of the newly discovered lands were ideal for the cultivation of sugar cane, a fact that Christopher Columbus noted immediately. On his second voyage to the Americas, Columbus brought cane cuttings from the Canary Islands and planted them on the island of Hispaniola (modern-day Haiti and the Dominican Republic), which the Spanish had claimed as their property.

Cultivating sugar cane was a difficult task. The conditions for growing it were so oppressive that for hundreds of years, most sugar cane was grown on plantations tended by slaves.

Unfortunately, as the European demand for sugar increased, so did the need for labor to produce it. The growing of sugar cane required hard labor in such brutally steamy climates that virtually no one would work voluntarily on a sugar plantation. At first, prisoners were imported to work as an alternative to being hanged. The Spanish also used the native people as slaves. The inhumane working conditions killed many of the workers, however, and the Europeans had to look for a new source of cheap labor. Hundreds of thousands of native Africans were captured and sold into slavery to work the plantations in Caribbean America to provide sugar for European tastes.

By the seventeenth century, sugar was by far the largest industry in the Caribbean, other parts of Central and South America, and as far north as the Gulf Coast of North America. This profitable venture brought great wealth to the countries of England and France, which oversaw much of the sugar production in this period.

ALTERNATIVES TO SUGAR CANE

In the mid-eighteenth century, European scientists discovered that a long-cultivated type of beet contained sucrose in sufficient quantities that it could be used as a source of sugar. Initially, the extraction process was too expensive and inefficient to compete with cane sugar. But during the Napoleonic Wars in the early nineteenth century, the powerful British fleet took firm control of the Caribbean and were able to cut off their French adversaries from their supplies of sugar. Under Napoleon Bonaparte, France responded by making a major effort to exploit sugar beets to replace cane sugar. Eventually, the methods were refined and beets became competitive with cane as a source of sugar.

World production of sugar has been growing at a steady rate ever since. The first sugar refinery in the United States was founded in 1689, and by the 1830s the U.S. had become a major player in the sugar industry. In 2003, the estimated annual yield of all sources of sugar worldwide exceeded 115 million tons, with about 30 percent of that beet sugar and

Truckloads of sugar beets await processing at a sugar plant.

Sugar was scarce during World War I. This poster encouraged people to use corn syrup as an alternative sweetener.

refinery: an industrial plant for purifying a substance such as sugar or oil

the other 70 percent cane sugar. In the meantime, scientists discovered ways to produce a liquid sweetener from corn. This product was made so cheaply and easily that corn syrup eventually replaced sugar as America's most common sweetener. Chemists have also developed a variety of low-calorie substances that provide a measure of sweetness without the calories of regular sugar.

SWEETS INDUSTRY

Over the centuries, people experimented with sugar and other sweeteners to create enticing food products. Bakers used sugar to produce delicious desserts. Cooks used it as a way to preserve fruit in the form of jellies and jams. The introduction of sugar to Great Britain in the sixteenth century greatly increased the consumption of tea, a relatively bitter beverage made more drinkable by the addition of sugar. An afternoon meal served with tea became a British tradition. Eventually, special chefs, who became known as confectioners, focused on creating snack products that were highly dependent on sugar. Technological improvements in the early nineteenth century helped turn confection making into a major industry, and by the mid-1800s, almost 400 American factories were producing candy and sweets.

confection: a sweet prepared food, such as candy. People who make or sell confections are called **confectioners**.

The sweets industry was unique in the business world because in virtually all cases success began on a very tiny scale. Most business owners started out in a family kitchen, usually with a secret formula or recipe that the entrepreneur developed on his or her own. Since there are a limited number of ways to mix the basic ingredients that make up most sweets, often the tiniest change in accepted ways of doing things created widely popular new products. For example, caramel was invented simply by adding milk to butterscotch. A New England homemaker invented peanut brittle in 1890 when she accidentally added baking soda instead of cream of tartar to a batch of peanut taffy she was making.

cream of tartar: a white acidic powder used in baking

From such modest beginnings, the sweets industry grew so huge that the smallest innovation could create large profits. In 2002, the United States candy market alone racked up more than $24.1 billion in sales. Yet the business is so cutthroat that hundreds of firms have gone out of business in recent years. From a high of more than 6,000 candy companies in the 1940s, only about 300 remained in 2003. Even among established companies, only a tiny percentage of new products that hit the market survive more than a few years.

Such high stakes mean that everyone in the industry is looking for an edge that will make the difference between riches and bankruptcy. These edges are hard to come by and are too valuable to be lost through carelessness. As a result, two of the prime characteristics of the sweets industry are secrecy and family control. Of the 300 companies in the United States that made candies in 2003, the vast majority were still private, family-owned companies, including the giant Mars company. The companies seldom gave interviews, and factory tours were almost unheard of. Some of them, such as the PEZ company of Connecticut, went to such lengths to preserve their secrecy that investigators had great difficulty determining who owned the company.

THE ENTREPRENEURS

Those who have succeeded in the world of sweets and treats are a colorful mixture of entrepreneurs with a wide range of strengths and weaknesses. Some of them, such as Milton Hershey, Frank Mars,

Invented in 1927 by Austrian Edward Haas, Pez was originally a breath mint sold in tins and marketed to adult smokers. Its name comes from a shortening of the word *Pfefferminz*, which is German for peppermint. The idea for using a dispenser was introduced in the late 1940s, although it was just a simple rectangular shape at the time. In 1952, Pez moved to the United States and changed its advertising focus to children. The company put heads on the dispensers and made the candies fruit flavored, thus creating the familiar candy and toy combination still loved by millions of adults and children today.

and Ben Cohen and Jerry Greenfield, were primarily craftsmen. Their main focus was on creating new and tasty treats, and they had little interest, experience, or expertise in any part of business. Some, such as Vernon Rudolph and Ellen Gordon, did not invent a new snack, but they were so astute at business that they built successful companies based on products created by other people. Others, such as William Wrigley Jr. and Wally Amos, were primarily salespeople. Their gifts lay not in creating a new food or in running a business, but in persuading customers to buy their products. And then there were the triple-threat operators, rare individuals such as Frank and Forrest Mars, who could create products, knew how to sell them, and were adept at operating a business.

The businesses these people ran may not be of vital national interest, nor will they have much effect on the futures of those who buy their wares. Nonetheless, the business builders in sweets and treats have created products that satisfy the cravings of the public so well that millions of loyal consumers are devoted customers from early childhood to the end of their days.

1

MILTON HERSHEY

DREAMS MADE OF CHOCOLATE

The deck was heavily stacked against Milton Hershey ever succeeding in life or in business. He grew up in poverty, torn between parents who constantly fought before they finally separated. He achieved, at best, a fourth-grade education and knew nothing about running a business. His main adviser, his father, was a hopeless dreamer who failed at every vocation he tried. As a candy maker, Hershey understood far less about the science of his craft than most of his competitors, relying almost exclusively on trial and error.

But Milton Hershey had two essential qualities that overrode all of his shortcomings: vision and luck. Hershey's father, Henry, had constantly preached, "If you want to make money, you must

Milton Hershey (1857-1945) and the candy company he built were a "rags to riches" success story. Hershey, however, measured his accomplishments by how much his money could do for others.

do things in a large way." Although that proved to be a recipe for disaster in Henry's life, it encouraged Milton to set his sights high and try to achieve what others would not dare attempt. A timely bit of luck with some caramels gave him the freedom to follow his dreams. This led him to create the world's first affordable chocolate bar, build an entire city on the foundation of his chocolate empire, and establish Hershey as the leading name in American chocolate manufacturing for more than a century.

A Miserable Childhood

Milton Snavely Hershey was born on September 13, 1857, on a farm in Hockersville, Pennsylvania. His mother, Fanny Hershey, was a strict Mennonite, one of a devout religious group that rejected the materialism and secularism of modern society. Milton's father, Henry, was a Mennonite in name only, as his primary goal in life was finding a way to get rich quick. During his lifetime, he tried at least 17 occupations and business ventures, including farming, oil drilling, writing, and inventing, and never made a living at any of them. Each failure left the family broke and forced them to travel to wherever Henry's next scheme took him. As a result of constant moving, Milton bounced from one school to the next, never staying long enough to learn the curriculum.

Henry Hershey's refusal to settle down with a responsible, steady vocation infuriated Fanny. She and Henry fought constantly. The relentless bickering, unsettled lifestyle, poverty, and the death of Milton's sister, Serena, from scarlet fever in 1867

Fanny Hershey in about 1918. Fanny disliked her husband so much she had herself listed as a widow in the Lancaster directory— while Henry was still alive and they were still married!

added up to a miserable childhood for Milton. Eventually, Fanny Hershey refused to follow Henry in his further quests for riches. The two separated and she did all she could to cut him out of her life. Determined that her son would make something of himself, Fanny tried to steer Milton into a trade that would provide a stable income. As he was barely literate, career opportunities were limited. In 1871, he became a printer's apprentice to the editor of a German-language newspaper in the town of Lancaster. Unfortunately, he lasted only three months there before being fired. Undaunted, Fanny arranged another apprenticeship for him in Lancaster, this time with Joseph Royer, a confectioner. Royer taught Milton that candy making was an art rather than a

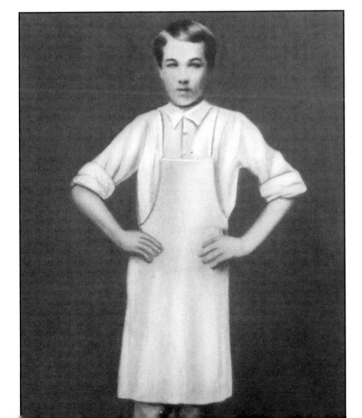

Milton Hershey, around 1873, while working as a confectioner's apprentice to Joseph Royer

science. He showed him how to determine "by feel" whether a batch was progressing as it should.

By the age of 19, Milton Hershey felt competent enough in the craft to start his own sweetshop in Philadelphia, with money borrowed from his aunt, Martha (Mattie) Snavely. Although he featured taffy as his main product, he also sold other candy, as well as ice cream, nuts, and fruits. Located in one of the nation's largest cities, his store did well enough that at one time he could afford to employ nine workers.

FATHER'S DISASTROUS ADVICE

In 1880, however, Henry Hershey reestablished contact with his son. Although Milton had already had more success in business than Henry had in his entire life, the elder Hershey viewed it as just a small beginning. He tried to interest Milton in manufacturing and selling a new type of medicated candy that Henry had invented and which he was certain would be a runaway success. Having caught wind of what Henry was up to, Fanny and her relations warned Milton against listening to Henry's advice.

Milton, who had long been torn by his parents' bitter marital battles and was by nature a kind, gentle man, felt caught in the middle. He tried to please his father by following some of his father's ideas, such as building elaborate display cases for his products. Unfortunately, this caused Milton to go dangerously into debt. Unable to handle the strain from the financial crisis and from trying to make peace between his parents, he suffered a nervous breakdown. After six years of making modest profits,

Henry Hershey around 1900. Henry was a creative man and an avid reader—but he was terrible at making a living for himself and his family.

Milton was forced to sell his business. Most of the money he received went to pay off debts.

When Hershey recovered from his illness, he decided he needed a change of scenery. With no other prospects on the horizon, he moved to Denver, Colorado, to join his father's latest adventure—mining silver. Henry Hershey had no more luck at this than at any of his other schemes, however, so Milton was forced to find work with a local confectioner. From this mentor, he learned how to make delicious caramels. The key, he discovered, was using fresh milk in the recipe.

The Hersheys soon gave up on Denver and moved to Chicago, where they went into business making Milton's caramels and Henry's cough drops. That lasted only a short period before Milton left in 1883 for New York City, where he found work with a candy manufacturer. After a long day at the factory, he would come home and work into the night making caramels, constantly trying to improve the recipe. Before long, he had saved enough money for another attempt at running a candy shop.

Again, just as before, things were going reasonably well until Henry showed up. Filled with business "wisdom" from his past failures, Henry was certain he knew how to make his son's shop a huge success this time. Convinced that his only mistake had been "that he was too timid," he persuaded Milton to manufacture cough drops along with his products and to spend large sums of money on rapid expansion. Again, Henry's advice led to disaster. In

1886, swamped in debt, Milton had to close his store. He left New York broke and discouraged.

HERSHEY'S BIG BREAK

Milton returned to Lancaster, where his mother and aunt agreed to take him in and support another candy effort, on one condition: that he have no more business dealings with his father. Milton agreed and returned to his kitchen, where, through constant experimentation, he produced an improved version of his caramels. He made the candies at night, Fanny and Aunt Mattie wrapped them, and Milton sold his sweets on the streets of Lancaster by day, carrying the candies around in a basket.

It was hard work that produced steady but modest income until Milton Hershey finally got his big break in 1887. An Englishman who was visiting Lancaster tasted one of Hershey's caramels and pronounced them the most delicious he had ever encountered. Certain that they would sell briskly in London, he placed a huge order for far more caramels than Hershey could possibly produce.

Recognizing this as the grand opportunity his father had futilely chased his entire life, Hershey begged bankers for a loan with which he could purchase ingredients and the machinery to manufacture the caramels in bulk. The local bankers, however, were painfully aware of the Hershey family's poor record when it came to business ventures and paying back loans, and they refused to extend him any credit.

Fortunately, one bank officer took a huge chance and personally provided Hershey with a short-term loan to get the order fulfilled. When the customer paid for the caramels, Hershey's financial problems were ended for good. He used the income to build a factory for mass production of caramels. Hershey's Lancaster Caramel Company proved to be an enormous success. By 1890, his caramels were selling so well that he added three more factories to keep up with the demand. Hershey was rich beyond his wildest dreams.

mass production: the manufacture of goods in large quantities

Hershey's success was based almost entirely on his superior product rather than any business savvy. According to one industry insider, "the only business concept Milton Hershey understood was product." He did not enjoy meetings or delving into the business operations of the company; as Lancaster Caramel grew, he hired experts and left them to handle the details of running the company. He had little interest in improving the efficiency of his operations or in finding ways to increase profit. All that counted for Hershey was making the most delicious candy. Even when he achieved such wealth that he did not have to work, he would show up in the company kitchens to experiment with new variations in his recipe or to personally teach employees his techniques of candy making.

AN EXOTIC NEW PRODUCT

Although he lived comfortably, Hershey was not an extravagant spender. He used his money to travel and sample sweets created by others. One such trip was to Chicago in 1893 to visit the Colombian Exposition. At this international fair, he came upon some chocolate candies made by a German manufacturer. Hershey loved the taste so much that he bought the entire display, including the chocolate-making equipment. From that moment, Hershey's interest in his caramels faded, and he became obsessed with chocolate. By the following year, he was ready to begin manufacturing chocolates.

While the chocolate industry was well established in Europe, few businesses in the U.S. had mastered the process. Hershey discovered that chocolate production was a far more complex operation than making caramels. Cacao beans have to be roasted and ground. The resulting liquid or powder is unsweetened chocolate. The chocolate is mixed with sugar, plus milk or flavors, then kneaded by a special machine for several days. Finally, the chocolate candy has to be slowly heated, then slowly cooled. Recognizing the extreme difficulty of the task, he hired two experienced chocolate makers to supervise the operation. The Hershey Chocolate Company started small, molding chocolate into novelty shapes, introducing some chocolate-coated caramels, and producing cocoa and unsweetened chocolate for home baking.

Hershey's top salesman and best friend, William Murrie, predicted that Americans would be unable to resist the new line of chocolate products. In 1895, he boldly declared to Hershey that he could sell more chocolate that year than Hershey could make—and then backed up his promise. While Hershey provided the vision for the company, Murrie was the one who carried it out and guided it to success. Responsible for running the company for more than

Connoisseurs agree that there are distinct national preferences in chocolate flavors. Americans prefer a harsher, grittier flavor like Hershey's; Italians like their chocolate bittersweet and dry; Germans enjoy a rich chocolate high in fat content; the British prefer a sweet, caramel-like taste; and Swiss chocolate has a strong aroma and silky smooth texture.

50 years, Murrie was described as "the only one who could tell Hershey no and get away with it."

For years, Hershey had been so engrossed in his candy business that he had little time for a social life. In 1898, however, the 40-year-old Hershey married Catherine (Kitty) Sweeney, who was more than 10 years his junior. The marriage created additional family problems for Hershey; his strong-willed mother did not approve of the marriage and refused to speak to Kitty. But despite the tension, he remained devoted to his wife.

Milton Hershey and his beloved Kitty in 1909

Discovering Chocolate

Chocolate, a product of the cacao tree, originated in the Americas with the Mesoamerican people. Archeological records show consumption of it as far back as 1000 B.C., and it was possibly used even earlier. The Mayan people called the beans from the cacao tree "food of the gods," and shared them during special ceremonies. The Aztecs considered cacao beans as valuable as gold or silver and used them as a form of currency. In addition to serving as money, the beans were also considered a culinary delicacy. They were first roasted and ground into a thick paste. The paste was then dissolved in water and flavored with spices. The resulting beverage, called chocolatl, was a privilege that only royalty could enjoy.

In 1502, while on a voyage to the New World, Christopher Columbus and his crew became the first Europeans to encounter the cacao beans. Although Columbus recognized that the beans were of great value to the local people, the Spanish for whom he sailed made no particular note of them. It wasn't until 1519, when explorer Hernando Cortes shared a cup of the bitter, frothy drink with Aztec emperor Montezuma, that Europeans really took an interest in the treat. Intrigued by the rich beverage, Cortes recorded the recipe and brought back cacao beans to Spain. There, he demonstrated how chocolate, when sweetened with sugar, made a delicious drink. The Spaniards kept this product a secret from other European nations for nearly 100 years, until word of it slowly began to spread across the continent. Eventually, chocolate drinks became a favorite of the wealthy—who were the only ones who could afford the extremely high price.

With an increase in cacao tree cultivation as well as the perfection of the steam engine (which assisted in the bean-grinding process), the price of chocolate gradually began to drop. By 1730, the flavorful beverage was readily available to most people. In 1828, the invention of the cocoa press helped make chocolate production even easier. In turn, as chocolate became more common, it began appearing in different forms with different purposes. Confectioners began to experiment with using chocolate as a flavoring in candies, and the first "eating chocolates" appeared in 1847.

In 1875, chocolatier Daniel Peter and chemist Henri Nestlé created milk chocolate. This invention was no small feat, since milk is 89 percent water and chocolate is 80 percent fat—and just as oil and water do not mix well, neither did milk and chocolate. (Plus, the butterfat found in milk tends to turn chocolate rancid.) The difficult nature of this task became readily apparent when Milton Hershey began working to devise his own method of milk-chocolate production.

At this point, Hershey had achieved his life's ambition. By 1900, his company was the largest manufacturer of caramels in the United States, employing 1,500 workers and topping $1 million in annual sales, and his chocolate products were providing an additional side income. Hershey became far more interested in spending time with Kitty than in managing the factories. On August 10, 1900, he sold the Lancaster Caramel Company for $1 million, along with his promise to stay out of the caramel business. He did, however, believe chocolate would one day be wildly popular, so he kept that part of the company. Letting Murrie oversee the day-to-day operations of the newly formed Hershey Chocolate Company, Milton took some time off to consider his next move.

BUILDING A CHOCOLATE UTOPIA

While debating what to do with the limitless possibilities that his fortune and free time provided, Hershey came up with an idea so elaborate that it reminded his dismayed family and friends of the eccentric schemes of his father. Unlike his father, however, Hershey's interest was not in making money—he had all that he needed—but in making a better world. He wanted to construct an ideal society "where the things of modern progress all center in a town that has no poverty, no nuisances, and no evil."

Hershey knew that such a town needed a business to support it and he proposed to center the entire venture on a new chocolate product—milk chocolate. For although his chocolate products were

Everyone, even Kitty, wondered about Milton's plans to build a utopian community. He never wavered in his vision, however. When asked how the town would help him turn a profit he always replied "I'm not out to make money. I have all that I need."

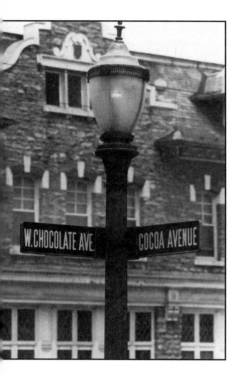

All the roads in Hershey, Pennsylvania, were given whimsical names such as these.

selling reasonably well, many people considered the flavor too strong and bitter. Furthermore, because of the intricate, complicated process and the expensive ingredients, chocolate items were a product for the wealthy or for special occasions when people really felt like splurging. Hershey had recently tasted some German milk chocolate and believed that with this product he could create something that no one else had ever achieved: a delicious chocolate bar that everyone could afford.

In order to accomplish this, Hershey had to pay attention to efficiency of production. Years before Henry Ford became famous as a pioneer in making products affordable through mass production, Hershey undertook a campaign to mass produce chocolate candy bars. He began scrapping many of the company's 114 chocolate products to concentrate on the milk-chocolate candy bar that would finance the construction of his ideal community.

In 1902, Hershey scouted much of the East Coast for an ideal location for his "Chocolate Town." Since fresh milk was such an important ingredient in milk chocolate, he sought to locate in a region of dairy farms. That led him back to his roots in Dauphin County, Pennsylvania. Hershey settled on a 1,200-acre parcel of land at a place called Derry Church, just a mile from his birthplace.

On March 2, 1903, construction began on a huge, modern chocolate factory. Hershey assisted in designing the factory as well as the layout of the town, including a downtown section and residential neighborhoods. (For example, he insisted the houses

have a variety of unique architectural styles, and wanted the factory made to be all on one floor to make it safer for employees in case of fire.) He initiated a contest to name his new town and declared Hersheykoko the winning entry. The United States postmaster, however, rejected the name as too commercial, and in 1906 the town's name was shortened to Hershey.

The Hershey factory in the early 1900s

THE SECRET OF MILK CHOCOLATE

So enthusiastic was Milton Hershey in constructing this ideal town that he got ahead of himself. For even as the chocolate factory and a creamery for processing the milk were being built, Hershey had no recipe for milk chocolate that was anywhere close to the German product he had tasted. Milk chocolate proved to be even more delicate than regular chocolate. Again, Hershey spent little time studying the European process. He simply rolled up his sleeves and began experimenting. After several years of trial and error and hundreds of failed attempts, he still had not mastered the craft. He and his chocolate makers could occasionally produce a decent batch, but more often than not, it came out burned or grainy or unblended. Hershey continued to struggle even as U.S. competitors such as Walter Baker were getting closer and closer to mastering the process of making milk chocolate.

One day, Milton Hershey inspected a vat filled with a silky milk solution that blended easily with the chocolate. The worker who created the solution, John Schmalback, was not one of Hershey's college-educated chemists, but a regular floor employee. Turning to him, Hershey exclaimed, "Look at that beautiful batch of milk! How come you didn't burn it? You didn't go to college!" Schmalback's breakthrough had been to dissolve a high concentration of sugar in the milk and then boil it slowly at low temperatures in a vacuum.

Now that he had a milk chocolate to use in his candy bar, Hershey could more rapidly phase out his other products and concentrate on mass-producing a few items. In addition to the milk-chocolate Hershey bar, Hershey added the penny-candy

"I climbed up on one of those giant mixers . . . and wouldn't you know, I fell in. I'll never forget that, swimming in that big vat of chocolate. Of course, my father got real angry, . . . but it was worth all of his yelling. How many boys do you know who get to dive into a river of chocolate?"
—Richard Murrie, son of Hershey president William Murrie, recalling a childhood visit to the factory

chocolate Kisses in 1907, and the chocolate-covered almond bar in 1908.

The Hershey Chocolate Company was the first candy company to succeed on a national level, and it did so by using every possible sales outlet it could find. Milton Hershey ordered his salespeople to "put the Hershey Milk Chocolate Bar on every counter, shelf, stand, and rack in every retail establishment in the U.S.—food store, restaurant, drug store, ice cream parlor and soda fountain."

Hershey's milk chocolate was a huge success. By 1907, the company's sales reached $2 million—double that of his caramel company at its peak. Four

One of the early ads for Hershey's Kisses. Originally Kisses were wrapped by hand, and the women who did the work were paid per piece (10 cents for every 20-dozen Kisses). This practice encouraged short-cuts. Some workers would lick the bottom of the Kiss to get the tissue paper flag to stick better. Otherwise, it had a tendency to slip out.

years later, total sales topped $5 million. The increased revenue allowed Hershey's ideal town to begin taking shape. In exchange for a 60-hour work week, employees were given economical housing and all the privileges of this planned community. By 1913, more than 700 people, most of them company employees, lived year-round in Hershey.

BITTERSWEET SUCCESS

Milton Hershey, however, found little enjoyment in watching his grand vision come alive. Kitty was in poor health most of the time, confined to her bed. Her condition worsened until she died in 1915.

With the love of his life gone, Hershey seldom returned to the town that carried his name. Instead, he spent most of his time in Cuba, where he embarked on another version of his utopian community. Hershey ended up controlling 65,000 acres (largely sugar fields) in Cuba, and he established a town, railroad, and school. He continued to look after the interests of his Pennsylvania chocolate company and community, but he was content to let his friend Murrie and others handle the operations. The company had evolved into a large business, about which Hershey had little knowledge or interest. "You do much better when I'm not around," he admitted to his company officers.

Indeed, Murrie and the others guided the Hershey Company into becoming the undisputed giant of the chocolate industry in the United States. This rise in prominence came in part from a large boost in sales during World War I. Prior to that

In 1925, Hershey introduced Mr. Goodbar, a milk-chocolate and peanut bar. In the 1930s it brought out Krackel and Hershey's Miniatures. Despite being introduced in the middle of the Great Depression, the candies sold well and are still popular today.

time, sales of the Hershey Milk Chocolate Bar were barely high enough to justify the mass-production system that Hershey had installed. The war, however, created a huge demand for a well-packaged, high-energy snack and the Hershey bar fit the bill perfectly. Soldiers liked their first tastes of this candy and returned from the war wanting more.

Over the years, Murrie greatly increased the efficiency of the Hershey factories and distribution systems. The company recorded sales of more than $41 million in 1929 and remained highly profitable through the Great Depression. World War II provided another boost to sales as Hershey supplied the U.S. armed forces with more than 1 billion bars during the conflict. Such sales volume allowed Hershey

Following World War I, Hershey developed the Field Ration D bar. This precursor to modern-day energy bars had 600 calories and could withstand temperatures of up to 120 degrees Fahrenheit. The ration bar was updated for the Gulf War in the early 1990s. The Desert Bar, as it was called, could withstand even higher temperatures and tasted better.

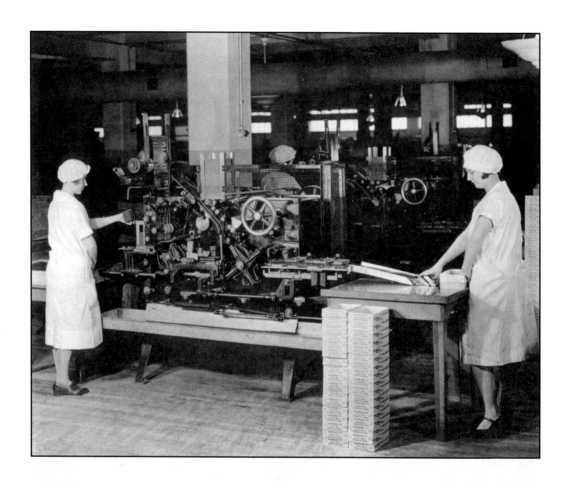

Although they look anti-quated now, in the 1920s and 1930s these wrapping machines were state of the art.

to build factories so massive and efficient that its rivals could not compete. By 1947, Hershey manufactured 90 percent of the milk chocolate in the United States. In fact, it actually supplied most of the chocolate used by rival candy-bar makers.

Murrie, however, was less successful in promoting Hershey's dream of an ideal, corporation-centered community. Although the town of Hershey grew to more than 2,500 residents in the 1930s, relations between employees and the company degenerated.

On April 2, 1937, 600 workers took over the factory buildings in a wage dispute. Five days later, they were violently thrown out by a group of angry farmers concerned that the work stoppage would cost them milk sales.

The violence so saddened Milton Hershey that he had little to do with the town thereafter. He spent much of his time experimenting with new products such as onion sherbet and cocoa butter soap, none of which was successful. Always a philanthropist,

Some of the striking workers being forcibly removed from the factory during the 1937 wage dispute. The workers had to make their way through a mob made up of angry farmers—many of whom tried to punch and kick them as they passed.

Hershey had given away his entire fortune during his lifetime. When he died of a heart attack in October 1945, he was essentially penniless.

LEGACY

Milton Hershey created the first inexpensive chocolate candy bar on the market. Although he knew and cared little about business management, he built his chocolate empire on two business techniques that have proved successful for many companies. First, he focused his efforts on a small line of products that he could mass produce. Such large-scale production lowered the cost of each individual candy bar, allowing him to sell his product for less. This, in turn, increased his share of the market.

The large scale of his operations then allowed for Hershey's second crucial business decision—to be the first confectioner to market his products nationally. Aided by the popularity of his candy bars with the armed forces, Hershey established the first brand name in chocolate recognized throughout the country. He was aided in this effort by his unique attempt to establish an ideal community. While Hershey, Pennsylvania, did not end up as a prototype for future communities, it served as a brilliant advertisement for Hershey's products. His "Chocolate Town" had a whimsical, fantasy quality that attracted millions of visitors and kept the name of Hershey before the public.

The company that Milton Hershey founded was by far the dominant chocolate company in the United States during most of the twentieth century.

In his later years, Hershey was a big fan of vegetables. In addition to onion sherbet, he also tried to make sherbet out of beets, celery, and carrots—all of which he swore were delicious. His perception may have been a bit skewed, however. In reality, after smoking as many as 10 cigars a day for 60 years, Hershey had completely burned out his taste buds and couldn't accurately taste a thing. None of his employees had the heart to tell him how awful the new inventions tasted.

Hershey acquired the H. B. Reese Candy company, makers of Reese's Peanut Butter Cups, in 1963. Since then, it has expanded the line to include Kit Kat bars, Reese's Pieces, and Nutrageous.

A modern Hershey employee performs a quality-control check to ensure that the Kisses measure up to the company's high standards.

After falling behind its rival, Mars, in sales in the 1970s, Hershey returned to the top spot with the acquisition of the distribution rights for candy giant Cadbury-Schweppes in 1988. In 2002, the company employed approximately 14,000 people worldwide and had an annual income of more than $4.1 billion. In addition to its traditional chocolate bar and Kisses, other popular Hershey brands included Kit Kat, Twizzlers, Jolly Rancher, and Carefree gum.

The legacy Milton Hershey would be proudest of, however, is that of the Hershey Industrial School. In 1909, the Hersheys, who were unable to have children of their own, set up a trust fund to found a school for orphaned boys. Inspired by his own lack of a dependable father figure, Hershey was determined to provide these boys with better childhoods than the one he had endured. "The biggest influence in a boy's life is what his dad does," said Hershey. "And when a boy doesn't happen to have any sort of a dad, he is a special mark. . . . I am afraid that most of our orphan boys have had a bad time of it. . . . They tell me that youngsters who go to prison never have a chance. Well, I am going to give some of them a chance my way." From this orphanage grew the Hershey Industrial School for disadvantaged children. Hershey had donated his entire estate to the school.

Just as Milton Hershey always intended, the profits from his chocolate helped contribute to making a better world. By 2005, his school had been renamed the Milton Hershey School and was the largest shareholder in the Hershey Corporation with billions of dollars in assets and control of 76 percent of the voting stock in the company. This money funded the education of more than 1,000 boys and girls each year. The majority of the students came from disadvantaged homes.

Milton Hershey and some of the boys from the Hershey Industrial School. In 1918, three years after Kitty's death, Milton gave the bulk of his vast personal fortune to the school. "If we had helped a hundred children it would have all been worthwhile," Hershey said.

2

WILLIAM WRIGLEY JR.

CHICAGO'S
CHEWING-GUM EMPIRE

William Wrigley Jr. provided an extreme example of the age-old business principle "the customer is always right." Wrigley started out selling soap only to find that, despite his skill and experience as a salesman, he could not get his customers excited about the product.

Instead of increasing his marketing efforts, Wrigley listened carefully to his customers and, based on what they told him, he scrapped his entire product line not once but twice. This unusually flexible attitude paid off in the end as, quite by accident, he found a product that earned him a fortune and made his name a household word throughout the United States.

William Wrigley Jr. (1861-1932) created a successful company with a little package of chewing gum and a huge talent for advertising.

THE CLASS TROUBLEMAKER

William Wrigley Jr. was born in 1861, in Philadelphia, Pennsylvania. He was the oldest, and by far the most difficult, of William Sr. and Mary Wrigley's eight children. After repeated scrapes with school authorities and his parents, he ran away from home at the age of 11. He rode a train to New York City, where he supported himself by selling newspapers and working as a cook's helper on ships docking at the harbor. For three months, he spent his nights sleeping in doorways and under wagons until the autumn weather grew too cold.

His adventure over, William returned to Philadelphia and went back to school, but his attitude had not changed. At the age of 12, he was permanently expelled from school for throwing a pie at the nameplate over the school entrance. Unlike William's classmates, his father was not amused by his behavior. "Your school life hasn't been a success," he said. "Let's see how work strikes you." William Sr. was a soapmaker, and he put his son to work in his factory, at the most tiring, monotonous job in the plant. For 10 hours a day, William Jr. stirred the soap in huge vats with a paddle.

Wrigley's salary for working in the soap factory? Six dollars a month.

SELLING SOAP

After a year of hard labor at the job, William was rewarded with a promotion to the company's sales staff. The 13-year-old drove a horse-drawn wagon filled with soap across rural Pennsylvania and into the population centers of New York and New

England in search of customers. From the beginning, it was clear that he had two of the key qualities of salesmanship: personality and persistence. William made friends wherever he went. No matter how desperate he was for a sale, he remained unfailingly polite and never argued with a customer. Over time, the goodwill he generated turned into sales.

William also discovered that patience was a virtue in this business. He was willing to spend whatever time and effort it took to seal the deal. On one occasion, a potential customer, after resisting William's sales pitch for two hours, finally sighed and said, "Well, sonny, I can see that I will have to buy some of your soap if I expect to do any business today."

William Wrigley Jr. began his business career selling his father's soap.

On another sales call, William camped on the doorstep of a large wholesaler in the middle of winter, waiting for a chance to see him.

Oddly, while William Wrigley Jr. could be tenacious on the doorstep of a customer, he did not show the same drive when it came to his overall career. He would lose interest in sales for a time, returning to the soap wagon only when he needed money. Nearly 17 years after first making the sales rounds for his father, he had made no progress in a career and had barely saved any money. If he were alone, it might have been fine, but in 1885 Wrigley had married Ada Foote and started a family.

In 1891, Wrigley left his father's company and moved westward to start his own business. He ended up in Chicago, where he set up shop as an independent salesman. Wrigley would contract himself out to companies who wanted him to sell their goods. The first product he sold was his father's soap. Although the elder Wrigley agreed to provide the initial product, the younger Wrigley was on his own in making his business grow. With only $32 in savings and a wife and child to support, he had to borrow nearly all the money he needed to get started selling soap wholesale to merchants, who then sold the soap in stores.

Wrigley married Ada Foote in 1885. They had two children, Phillip and Dorothy.

LISTENING TO THE CUSTOMER

From the start, Wrigley made a practice of listening to his customers. When the local merchants complained that they could not make any money charging the low price set for the product, Wrigley took them seriously. He raised the price on a box of soap, and then set about finding a way to entice consumers into buying his soap despite the markup.

The sales technique he decided to use to do this was the premium—giving something away to each customer who bought his soap. The key was finding an item attractive to customers yet inexpensive enough that he could afford to give it away. Wrigley managed to obtain a large stock of red umbrellas at a low cost and used them as his first premium. The sales promotion proved so popular that Wrigley made it a cornerstone of his marketing strategy. "Everyone likes something extra, for nothing," he concluded.

When the umbrellas ran out, Wrigley negotiated a good deal on a huge quantity of baking powder to give away with the soap. Before long, he discovered that customers seemed more interested in the baking powder than in the soap. Wrigley, who never argued with a customer, viewed the situation not as a business setback, but rather as an opportunity. If baking powder was what people wanted, baking powder was what he would give them. To make the customers happy, he added baking powder to his line of products. Wrigley then searched for an attractive giveaway item. He tried cookbooks and various toiletries, but the product he finally settled on was chewing gum, which he purchased from the Zeno Company.

Not long after the promotion began, Wrigley became aware of a familiar trend. Customers were contacting him, asking if they could get more gum

A Brief History of Chewing Gum

People have chewed on gum-like substances for thousands of years. The ancient Greeks chewed a gum made from the resin of mastic trees. Mayan people chewed on chicle—the latex sap from sapodilla trees, which can be found in much of Central America. Later, in North America, Native Americans cut and chewed the gum-like resin from spruce trees. This tradition was passed on to white settlers, with whom it became quite popular. By the early 1800s, lumps of spruce gum were being sold as the first commercial chewing gum.

In the 1860s, the former president of Mexico, General Antonio Lopez de Santa Anna, had been exiled from his country and was staying with a young friend of his, Thomas Adams, in New York City. One day, Santa Anna mentioned how chicle, a common product in his native Mexico, might be a good way for Adams to make some extra money. Santa Anna thought that Adams might be able to figure out a way to blend chicle with rubber in order to make a new and improved tire for carriages and bicycles.

Adams thought this was a good idea, and he bought a large shipment of Mexican chicle and began tinkering with the mixture. Unfortunately, he was never able to figure out how to produce a better tire. Nor was he able to use the substance to improve rain boots, children's toys, or costume masks. Just when the investment was beginning to seem like a waste of money, however, Adams came up with something promising. In 1875, he formally introduced his new product: Adams' New York Gum No. 1, an unflavored, chicle-based chewing gum. It was the first of its kind and a pleasant alternative to the crumbly, paraffin-wax-based gums then available. Sales of New York No. 1 were brisk, and the treat rapidly grew in popularity.

The success of his gum convinced Adams to try and produce a flavored gum. This posed a problem, because the chicle-based product alone wouldn't hold the flavor for more than a minute. It wasn't until 1880 that popcorn salesman William J. White discovered that by adding sugar and corn syrup to the mix, he could get chewing gum to retain its flavor. White went on to market Yucatan, a successful peppermint gum. In 1899, White and Adams became president and chairman, respectively, of the newly founded American Chicle Company.

Although it could be found nationwide, chewing gum remained more or less a novelty until the arrival of William Wrigley Jr. When he hit the scene in the beginning of the 1910s with his inventive marketing techniques, the popularity of chewing gum soared.

without having to buy the baking powder. By the end of 1892, Wrigley had discontinued his main product and again moved into sales of the premium. At first he used two of Zeno's brands: Vassar, which was marketed to women, and Lotta Gum, advertised to the general public. At the same time, however, he was also experimenting with his own brands of chicle-based gum. In 1893, he came up with two flavors, Spearmint and Juicy Fruit, and packaged them in units of five individually wrapped sticks with the Wrigley name boldly emblazoned on the package.

This display features Wrigley chewing gum packages from early in the company's existence.

With missionary zeal and a firm commitment to his product, Wrigley set about making his gum nationally known. In 1893, he spent 187 nights in railroad sleeping cars as he crossed the country promoting his new products.

Wrigley still believed that premiums were the best way to attract new customers. This time, he tried to build goodwill among store owners and food and snack distributors by offering more expensive items such as cash registers and coffeemakers to those who bought large quantities of gum. He also made the shrewd observation that consumers seldom planned a purchase of gum—more often they bought it on the spur of the moment. To increase the chances of an impulse purchase, he created display cases to set up near cash registers so customers could add a pack of gum to the purchases for which they were already paying.

The Spearmint and Juicy Fruit brands sold so well that Wrigley quickly discontinued the Vassar and Lotta Gum brands. Occasionally, he would branch out into new and exotic flavors such as Blood Orange and Lemon Creme, but such experiments were generally short-lived.

Wrigley's relations with his competitors were often strained. In 1899, he was invited to join with six other gum manufacturers in a cooperative effort to promote their products. Wrigley refused and instead engaged in an aggressive campaign to win customers for himself. His competitors took up his challenge, and before long all of them were spending far more money than they could afford on advertising. Wrigley's campaign nearly ruined him. His ads failed to increase his small share of the national gum market, and when an economic depression swept the country in 1907, putting many people out of business, Wrigley was nearly bankrupt.

WRIGLEY'S BOLD GAMBLE

Although William Wrigley was in grave danger of losing his business, he was not the sort to panic. One of his associates once remarked, "I've never seen Mr. Wrigley flustered; I've never even seen him act worried. He just seems to approach everything in an easy, uncomplicated way."

In fact, Wrigley chose this low point in his business career to launch his most outrageously daring scheme yet in an attempt to increase his small share of the national gum market. While his competitors responded to the economic slump and reduced revenues by cutting expenses until the bad times were over, he did just the opposite. Because so many businesses were afraid to spend money, newspapers and magazines were forced to slash their advertising rates dramatically in order to attract any business. William Wrigley saw this as a unique opportunity to purchase a flood of advertising for very little cost. "Tell 'em quick and tell 'em often" was his marketing motto, and he took out a staggering loan of $250,000 to pay for a massive ad campaign. Despite being almost broke, he took on a debt that was greater than his entire sales for a year just to advertise his

During his career, Wrigley bought advertising space on 62,000 street and subway cars.

Wrigley's mile-long sign was one of the company's most famous ads.

product. If the ad campaign did not produce spectacular results, his company was doomed.

Wrigley's relentless barrage of ads, combined with his competitors' silence as they sat cautiously on the sidelines, gave the nation the impression that there was only one major national manufacturer of gum. When shoppers reached for a pack of gum, Wrigley's was the only name they recognized, and they were far more likely to buy a familiar brand than an unknown brand. At the same time, Wrigley devised an ingenious way to make contact with thousands of retailers. Falling back on his favorite sales strategy of giving the customer something for nothing, his advertisements included coupons that entitled retailers to free boxes of Spearmint gum from his distributors. When the retail store owners showed up to claim their gifts, the distributors were able to add them to their list of potential customers.

Wrigley's advertising gamble and giveaway strategy paid off handsomely. In a little more than a year, the company's annual sales skyrocketed from $170,000 to more than $3 million. By 1910, Spearmint gum was the nation's best-selling brand, followed closely by the Juicy Fruit label.

Not content to rest with this accomplishment, Wrigley looked for creative ways to solidify his hold on the gum market. In 1914, he introduced Doublemint gum, for which he eventually created a memorable image by using twins in many ads for the product. He also continued to give the public "something for nothing." Reasoning that those people who could afford a telephone would also be able to afford to spend money on gum, he collected copies of all the phone directories in the United States in 1915. He then mailed a free four-stick pack of Wrigley's gum to each of the 1.5 million

Around the same time Wrigley introduced Doublemint, Milton Hershey also began manufacturing mint chewing gum. Sold with a bonus sixth stick in every pack, the product was initially a competitor for Wrigley. Restrictions on sugar imports in the years following World War I, however, made it difficult for Hershey to supply both his gum and his chocolate lines, and the product was discontinued in 1924.

51

Be Healthy-Happy-Wise
Enjoy Delicious
Double Mint Gum

WRIGLEY'S
DOUBLE MINT
CHEWING GUM

Aid Teeth
Breath—Digestion Daily
...Millions Do

This Doublemint gum ad from 1938 was one of the few that didn't use twins.

Wrigley's campaign to send free gum to every listing in the U.S. phone books was likely the first example of direct marketing. This strategy of appealing to potential customers through mass mailings has become a standard sales tool for thousands of businesses today.

addresses listed in the directories. Wrigley repeated the practice in 1919, when the list of telephone subscribers had grown to more than 7 million.

WRIGLEY MAKES IT BIG

In gaining control of the rapidly growing U.S. gum market, Wrigley became a wealthy man, and he further increased his wealth with a series of astute business moves. In 1919, he opened his company to public ownership on the stock market, which brought him millions of dollars. Wrigley invested much of his money in real estate. He made a wise purchase in 1919 when he paid $3 million for a large part of Catalina Island, located off the California coast near Los Angeles. As Los Angeles grew into a major metropolitan area and land values soared, his resorts on the island became worth many times what he originally paid. Wrigley also invested in mining, hotels, railroads, and a baseball team—the Chicago Cubs. (In 2005, more than 80 years after Wrigley purchased the team, the Cubs were still playing at the ballpark named in his honor.)

Wrigley earned enough profit ($8.5 million by 1921) that he could afford to take a long-range view of his company. When asked the secret of his success, Wrigley once responded, "Restraint in regard to immediate profits. That has not only been our most profitable policy, it has been pretty nearly our only profitable one." He saw that in the long run, Wrigley gum could hold its dominance in the marketplace if he kept prices low, even at the expense of profits. As a result, the Wrigley company compiled a record, virtually unmatched among snack and food companies, of holding the line on prices. The first major increase in the price of a pack of gum did not come until 1971.

Wrigley was so energized by his business that he arose at five o'clock every morning and went to work. After founding his gum company, he never took a vacation that did not also involve business. He died in 1932, at which time his son Phillip took over the company. The company faced only one major crisis following his death—its source of chicle was cut off during World War II when the Japanese controlled the Pacific Ocean. What little gum it was able to produce was earmarked for the armed forces, not the general public. Phillip Wrigley, however, proved that he had learned much from watching his father. His company openly admitted that its substitute product was greatly inferior to its regular gum. Wrigley took out ads featuring an empty Spearmint wrapper and the words "Remember this wrapper!" and then took the product off the civilian market. Americans did remember the wrapper, and the wartime loss of sales was quickly erased by a tremendous boost in demand once supplies came back at the war's end.

LEGACY

By the time of William Wrigley Jr.'s death in 1932, his company stood unchallenged as the dominant manufacturer of gum in the United States. And in the twenty-first century, after more than 110 years of doing business, the Wm. Wrigley Jr. Company retained its firm grip on the market. Still under the leadership of the Wrigley family, it continued to manufacture nearly half of all the gum sold in the country. In 2002, led by Bill Wrigley Jr., great-grandson of William Wrigley Jr., the company recorded net sales of more than $2.7 billion.

William Wrigley Jr. pioneered a number of market strategies that were widely copied over the years. He was perhaps the first U.S. entrepreneur to fully recognize the potential of mass advertising. Despite selling a small, inexpensive product, Wrigley spent more money on advertising during his lifetime than any other single-product manufacturer in the world—more than $100 million between 1892 and 1932. He discovered that the ads were worth every penny he put into them. By restricting his product line, Wrigley was able to concentrate the power of

Wrigley was generous with his money. He was the first employer to give Saturdays off, and his employees were provided benefits such as free medical care, life insurance, and free manicures and shampoos for the female workers.

The first person to use commercial jingles on the radio was William Wrigley Jr.

those ads on just a few items. In the twenty-first century, the Wrigley company continued to thrive on sales of its longtime standard-bearers, Spearmint, Juicy Fruit, and Doublemint. Other popular products included Big Red and Eclipse, as well as the successful Extra line of sugar-free gums.

Finally, William Wrigley Jr. used the profits from his company to create a lasting legacy for himself in the city of Chicago. In 1924, he constructed the Wrigley Building, which has stood as a landmark in the city since. In 2005, his Chicago Cubs were still one of the nation's most popular sports teams, and the ballpark in which they played, Wrigley Field, was one of the most famous and beloved sports facilities in the country.

In order to make the flavoring for its Spearmint gum, the Wrigley company grows enough mint in the U.S. alone to fill more than 16,300 football fields.

The Wm. Wrigley Jr. Company headquarters were housed in the striking white Wrigley building, located on Michigan Avenue in Chicago, Illinois.

3

FRANK AND FORREST MARS

THE FIRST FAMILY OF CANDY

When the children of Forrest Mars were growing up, their father refused to let them eat any of the M&M's candies that his company produced. He told them the company couldn't spare any of the small candy pieces, so they had to do without. The claim was ludicrous, given the company's handsome profits. But at least that was an improvement over a decade earlier, when the same children had to go without food of any kind so the money could go to their father's business. In that regard, Forrest was carrying on the dubious tradition of his own father, Frank Mars, who was so obsessed with getting a business up and running that his wife sent young

The Mars family members were extremely private and reluctant to speak with the media or be photographed. This Yale college yearbook photo of Forrest Mars (1904-1999) is from 1928.

Forrest to live with her parents in Canada for fear he would starve if he stayed.

Such intense focus on the business, together with some innovative products, drove the Mars company as it competed for the title of the world's largest candy manufacturer, and it also made the succeeding Mars generation one of the richest families in the world.

A ROCKY START

The man who started it all, Frank Mars, was born on September 24, 1883, in Pennsylvania. When he was young, his family moved to St. Paul, Minnesota, where Frank's father found work as a gristmill operator. As a young child, Frank developed polio (an infectious disease that can cause paralysis and muscle shortening and distortion), which kept him from playing with other children. Because of this, he spent much of his time in the kitchen with his mother, who was an excellent cook. One of the skills she taught him was the art of making candy, and Frank enjoyed experimenting with his own recipes.

Upon leaving high school, Mars decided to start a wholesale candy company in Minneapolis. Instead of making his own candy, however, he was content to sell penny candy made by his suppliers—women working in their own kitchens. In 1902, while Mars was struggling to keep his small business afloat, he married Ethel Kissack. Two years later, their only child, Forrest, was born.

Frank Mars worked hard to build his business, to the point where he used almost all of his earnings on expenses such as supplies and travel. Rent bills went unpaid and the cupboards were bare of food, but Frank seemed not to notice. Ethel feared for the survival of their son. In 1910, she divorced Frank and, unable to care for her child while supporting herself as a clerk at a downtown department store, sent Forrest to live with her parents in a small mining town in Saskatchewan, Canada.

Despite Frank Mars's penny-pinching, he finally had to abandon his floundering business. Remarried to another woman named Ethel, he moved to Seattle to try his luck manufacturing and selling his own candy. Again, he lived in squalor while pumping all his money into the business, but he went bankrupt. Mars made a third attempt at the candy business in Tacoma, Washington, but the company lasted only a short time before going out of business in 1914.

IF AT FIRST YOU DON'T SUCCEED. . . .

Stubbornly refusing to consider a less risky career, Mars returned to the Twin Cities of Minneapolis and St. Paul to try yet again. His past failures, however, came back to haunt him. In light of Mars's bankruptcy history, no one would give him any supplies unless he paid for them in cash. Mars had to make do with scavenging small quantities of surplus ingredients from other candy makers. He and Ethel lived in a small room above a kitchen, where Frank cooked a fresh batch of candy each day. Ethel would take whatever he had made and sell it on the trolleys. Mars's favorite creation was a mixture of caramel, nuts, and chocolate that he named the Mar-O-Bar, but his best-selling confection was his Victorian Butter Creams, made from a recipe he had learned in Seattle.

This time Mars's business prospered. He eventually moved out of his kitchen into a small factory, and he gradually expanded his sales territory as far east as Chicago. In 1922, he incorporated his business. With clients such as retail-store giant Woolworth signing contracts with him for regular candy deliveries, Mars was assured of steady sales and a handsome living.

REUNION

In the meantime, Forrest Mars spent his childhood far away in Canada. He had no contact with his father and knew little about him beyond his mother's description of Frank as "that miserable failure." An excellent student, Forrest completed high school in 1922 at Lethbridge, Alberta, and earned a scholarship to the University of California at Berkeley, where he planned to study mining engineering.

While in college, Forrest found he could earn considerable spending money as a salesman. During the summer of 1923, he traveled across the country selling Camel cigarettes. An aggressive salesman, he plastered Camel posters all over the Chicago shopping district, an illegal activity that drew the wrath of shopkeepers. Forrest was arrested and put in jail. By fortunate coincidence, his father happened to be in town on business; he stunned Forrest by coming down to jail to bail him out.

Forrest was further amazed to learn that Frank was a wealthy business owner. The two discussed business for a while and Frank asked Forrest if he had any interest in joining the company. Forrest was still committed to school, but he had come to enjoy the world of sales. He would not mind selling for his father if they could come up with a product that he could sell all over the United States, as he was doing for Camel cigarettes.

THE MALTED-MILK CHOCOLATE BAR

With more than 65 percent of his sales concentrated in the Twin Cities, Frank was not ready to go national with his candy. At that time, the giant Hershey Chocolate Company, with its huge factory, wealth, sales force, reputation, and unique milk-chocolate product, was the only company able to market candy across the country. Frank knew he was not in the same league.

According to Forrest, as they discussed the situation over malted milks, an idea suddenly occurred to him. "Why don't you put this chocolate malted drink into a candy bar?" he suggested. Whether it was father or son who actually came up with the idea, Frank Mars soon developed a new candy bar with a whipped chocolate filling encased in a solid coat of chocolate that kept the inside ingredients fresh. The bar, which he named Milky Way, proved to be a runaway success, earning over $800,000 in sales in 1924—its first year of production.

In creating the Milky Way, the Mars men stumbled upon a product with immense appeal that had

The creamy malted milk inspired Frank and Forrest Mars to create the Milky Way candy bar.

The twenty-first century version of the Milky Way was about the same size as its competitors, but still featured the malted-milk-flavored inside.

little to do with its flavor. The sugary filling, known in the industry as a nougat, was far cheaper to produce than chocolate. Yet when the bar was surrounded by chocolate coating, customers had the impression that they were looking at a chocolate bar. As a result, Mars could afford to make a much larger bar than chocolate-bar manufacturers could. When placed side by side with its competition, the Milky Way always looked like a bargain.

BEYOND THE MILKY WAY

While Frank Mars was growing wealthy on Milky Way bars, Forrest continued his education. He moved across the country from the University of California to Yale University. Giving up on mining, he planned to study economics. At Yale, he learned a great deal about running a large business, not only from his classes, but also by asking questions of his roommate, the nephew of chemical-industry tycoon Pierre DuPont. Meanwhile, he again proved his sales expertise by making a fortune peddling ties in the school cafeteria.

After completing college, Forrest was ready to join his father at the company's new headquarters in Chicago. Mars Inc. was now a booming business—in 1929, thanks largely to the popularity of Milky Way, it produced 20 million candy bars. The following year, Frank achieved even greater success with the invention of the peanut, caramel, nougat, and chocolate bar that he called Snickers, after one of his favorite horses. Snickers quickly caught on. Eventually, it would surpass the Hershey milk-chocolate bar as the top-selling candy bar in the United States, a rank it retained into the twenty-first century.

In 1932, Frank created yet another innovative treat, which he called Three Musketeers because it consisted of three flavored nougat pieces (chocolate, vanilla, and strawberry) coated in chocolate. When the price of strawberries rose drastically a short time later, Mars abandoned the three flavors and went with all chocolate centers, but retained the name.

A Three Musketeers bar

Mars's growing line of popular bars totaled more than $25 million in sales in 1932, making the company the second-ranked candy manufacturer in the

Many candy manufacturers still dipped chocolates by hand in the 1930s.

nation. But while Frank Mars basked in those sales figures and enjoyed wealth beyond his expectations, Forrest constantly searched for new ways to make the company even more successful. He oversaw construction of a new state-of-the-art factory in Chicago and urged his father to expand aggressively to challenge Hershey. He made a nuisance of himself, interfering with the work of supervisors, administrators, and workers, and his arguments with his father grew more heated. Finally, in the fall of 1932, Frank could take no more. He pushed Forrest out of the company, giving him $50,000 and the foreign rights to manufacture Milky Way as a parting gift. Forrest left for Europe with his wife, Audrey, and their child, Forrest Jr. He would never see his father again; Frank Mars died 15 months later of kidney failure.

NEW BEGINNINGS

At first, Forrest wanted a clean break from the bitter memories of the candy-bar business, and he began selling shoe racks in Europe. But within a few months, he decided to get back into the business—this time running a company on his own terms. It had constantly rankled him that Mars had to depend on Hershey for the chocolate coating on its candy bars instead of learning how to manufacture chocolate itself. What sense did it make, Forrest asked, to support the company's largest competitor by purchasing one-fifth of all the chocolate that Hershey made? "If you want to get rich, you gotta know how to make a product," he said. "And you aren't going to hire anybody to make a product for you to make you rich."

With that in mind, Forrest set out to solve that weak link in his father's business—the art of making chocolate. He hired on as an ordinary factory worker for two renowned Swiss chocolate manufacturers: Tobler and Nestlé. (The ease with which he was able to learn their secrets contributed to his later obsession with secrecy in his own plants.)

Frank's Chicago factory was not only state of the art, it was also attractive. It was designed to look like a Spanish-style monastery, and nothing on the outside of the building even hinted that there was a manufacturing business on the inside. The *Chicago Tribune* said it was so appealing-looking it actually boosted home sales in the area.

In its early years, the Hershey Company made much of its money by selling its chocolate to other candy companies. In 1921, the company was selling about 8.3 million pounds of chocolate a year. By 1938, it was selling 8.4 million pounds a month—thanks in large part to Mars. Before the companies parted ways, Mars was one of Hershey's biggest customers, accounting for a fourth of Hershey's chocolate output and 20 percent of its total sales.

Having learned what he could, Mars moved to England in 1933 to start a company in a country where he spoke the language. Like his father, he started making candy in his kitchen, primarily a version of the Milky Way that he called the Mars Bar. Faced with stiff competition from large, well-established English candy firms such as Cadbury Brothers, Limited, and Rowntree & Company, Mars repeated his father's behavior of pouring all of his energy and money into business at the expense of everything else. After enduring months of shivering in their unheated, one-room apartment with barely any food to eat, his wife and son departed for the United States.

Unlike his father, Forrest did not restrict his business to candy. "I'm not a candy-maker," he once noted. "I'm empire-minded." After he discovered that few companies in England produced food for pets, he purchased a small dog-food company in 1934—despite the danger of having his candy's reputation tarnished by association with such a product. While his candy-bar business was still catching on, he increased his company's sales of dog food five times in just five years to become Great Britain's largest pet-food manufacturer. Eventually, Mars's extra-large, chocolate-covered nougat candy bars also won over customers, and by 1939, Mars Ltd. had grown to become Great Britain's third-largest candy manufacturer.

By the time Forrest Mars's candy company really started to take off, however, Great Britain was at war with Nazi Germany. Needing money to finance its military, the government levied high taxes on all foreign residents. Rather than pay the taxes, Mars abandoned the country and returned to the United States, leaving his company in the hands of his top British manager, Colin Pratt.

Mars took with him an idea for a candy completely different from those upon which his family had made its fortune. Most stores greatly cut back on their orders of chocolate during the summer months because it melted in the heat. But while traveling in Spain during the Spanish Civil War of the late 1930s, Mars had encountered soldiers eating small pieces of chocolate even in the warmest weather. The chocolate was coated with a hard, sugary candy to keep it from melting. Mars planned to introduce a similar candy to the United States, but he needed both a source of chocolate and a financial backer for the project.

It just so happened that Mars's largest competitor in the United States, the Hershey Company, could supply both. Although it was against his principles for business success, Mars decided to initially enlist the support of his rival. On a steamy August day, he arranged to call on Hershey's top executive, William Murrie, carrying a sample of his new candy in his pocket. When Mars produced the candies unaffected by heat that would have made a mess of most chocolate products on the market, Murrie was impressed. He was even more pleased that Mars was offering to produce the candies in partnership with Murrie's son Bruce, and had even offered to share top billing for the candy's name by calling them "M&M's," for "Mars and Murrie."

With an enthusiastic Bruce Murrie on board, M&M Ltd. opened for business in 1940. Hershey not only provided materials and money, but also brought in its engineers to help design and install the necessary equipment. Soon, however, Murrie discovered that Mars had no interest in him as a business partner. All Mars had wanted was Murrie's important connections. Mars paid no attention to Murrie's ideas on running things and treated him so shabbily that Murrie eventually quit the company in frustration. But by then, M&M's was firmly established as a profitable product.

TAKING AIM AT HERSHEY

Forrest Mars continued to seek out ways to expand his business empire outside of candy. In 1942, he learned of a new rice milling technique that allowed the rice to retain more nutrients. He bought the rights to this new technology and formed a company to manufacture and sell the rice, which he called Uncle Ben's. At the same time, he tried to reestablish his connection with his father's candy company. Mars's stepmother, who retained a large share of control in the business following her husband's death, thwarted him for several years. But upon her death in 1945, Forrest inherited half her

The model for Uncle Ben was an affable waiter who served lunch to Forrest Mars and ad executive Leo Burnett at a Chicago restaurant in 1943. The two were discussing what to call Mars's new brand of rice when Burnett pointed to their server and said, "If you want everybody eating your rice, you better have somebody real friendly like him serving it." Mars offered the waiter $50 to sit for a portrait. The man agreed and also consented to giving Mars the rights to the picture, and the face of Uncle Ben was born.

stock in the company and claimed a seat on its board of directors. This put him in a position to begin a bitter battle with management over control of the company, a fight he finally won in 1964.

Mars's interest in his father's company, combined with the profits of M&M's, earned him millions. Yet he was not happy. His goal was not merely to be financially successful, but to be the best and largest candy company in the world. Mars's driven nature made him, at times, an overbearing taskmaster. He expected his managers to be on call day and night. One time, for example, Mars purchased a bag of his own candy at a convenience store and found that the corner of the letter "M" on a few of the M&Ms was slightly faded. He called the plant manager at home at 3:00 A.M. and demanded a recall on that particular batch of candies. And if any person or department failed to meet production goals or allowed the tiniest lapse in quality control, Mars unleashed an explosive fit of temper. "I don't think I've ever seen anybody carry on the way he [could]. I mean, I didn't know it was possible to yell for that long," said one of his associates.

On the other hand, Mars rewarded hard work handsomely. He paid his employees far more than the industry average, offered bonuses and incentives for meeting goals, and tied salaries to the company's overall performance. He also made a point of treating all his employees with equal respect (or lack of it). There was little room for bureaucracy or middle managers in Mars's system. He disdained the use of memos and preferred face-to-face communication. Upper management was allowed few privileges, and all employees were given heavy responsibility.

In 1950, Mars hired a consultant to create an advertising campaign for M&M's. This campaign made use of cartoon characters to appeal to children, and the slogan "melts in your mouth, not in your hand" to appeal to parents. Mars then aired the ads on children's television shows. This created such a demand for the product that by 1956, M&M's was earning $40 million a year in sales, making it the most popular single candy item on the market.

At the same time, Mars pushed for modernization of equipment and procedures. In 1953, the company switched to a completely mechanized, continuous-flow system of producing its traditional candy bars. By 1959, the retooling of the company's factories was complete, resulting in a process so streamlined that Mars Inc. could produce almost 30 times more candy bars in one day than it could before.

Mars continued a lifelong policy of living modestly and putting most of his considerable earnings back into the company. By 1964, he was able to

Periodically, Mars changed the distribution of colors in its bags of M&Ms. In 2005, the mix was 30 percent brown, 20 percent each of yellow and red, and 10 percent each for orange, blue, and green.

Snickers remained Americans' favorite candy bar in 2005.

gain ownership of the entire Mars enterprise. A year later, he made the break he had long been plotting by notifying Hershey that Mars would be phasing out its purchasing of Hershey's chocolate coating. The era of cooperation among the large candy manufacturers was over, and an intense battle that reflected Forrest Mars's competitive nature ensued.

In 1973, Mars retired from the company that bore his name, leaving it in the hands of his sons, Forrest Jr. and John. Their sister, Jackie, joined them a few years later. Forrest Sr.'s retirement did not last long, however, as he founded Ethel M. Chocolates and oversaw its daily operations for the next 10 years. Forrest Mars Sr. died on July 1, 1999, at age 95.

LEGACY

Frank and Forrest Mars created some of the most beloved candy snacks of all time. At the beginning of the twenty-first century, M&M's continued to rank as the most popular candy item in the world. The company's plant in Hackettstown, New Jersey, produced more than 100 million M&M's pieces every eight-hour shift, and the candy generated more than $2 billion in annual sales. Meanwhile, Snickers remained the favorite candy bar in the United States. Some of Mars's other well-known food products included Twix, Skittles, and Uncle Ben's Rice. In addition, Mars controlled a large portion of the pet-food market with its popular brands of Pedigree, Whiskas, Cesar, and Sheba. Including its pet food, snack food, and regular food lines, the company had more than 70 divisions and 28,000 employees worldwide.

Mars initiated the bitter contest for bragging rights with Hershey that has dominated the U.S. candy market in recent decades. Industry experts have described the competition between the two as one of the fiercest in the business world. Their battles have frequently led to public accusations of corporate misdeeds, as well as lawsuits over business practices. Determined to keep their secrets from competitors, the Mars employees guard the company's privacy jealously. Workers virtually never speak publicly or grant interviews, and security at all their plants is a top priority.

In the United States retail industry, chocolate brings in $13 billion annually.

From a business standpoint, Mars achieved an advantage over competitors by accepting a far lower profit margin, by constantly reinvesting profits in the company rather than in executive perks or a luxurious lifestyle, and by a relentless drive for efficiency of operations. The Mars company finally surpassed Hershey as the top candy manufacturer in the United States in the early 1980s, only to have Hershey regain the lead in 1988 with the purchase of the manufacturers of Almond Joy and Mounds candy bars. Mars, however, concentrated more on the global market, increasing its world sales from $800 million annually in 1973 to more than $14 billion by 2003, and it continued to lead Hershey in world sales. The Mars family has profited phenomenally from their diverse business. Their fortune is estimated to have surpassed $10 billion, making them one of the wealthiest families in the world.

Each year, Americans eat more than 25 pounds of candy per person.

4
VERNON RUDOLPH

KRISPY KREME DOUGHNUTS: HOTTEST BRAND GOING

Radio disc jockeys count down the hours until their arrival in town. A television station hires a helicopter to rush them to a promotional location. Mobs of fans stand in line in the early morning darkness, braving the cold while waiting for the doors to open so that they can be the first on their block to greet America's latest sensations.

The object of all this fan frenzy is not a new rock group or the latest teen heartthrob movie star. Rather, it is a doughnut. Krispy Kreme has opened a new store and thousands of salivating customers cannot wait to bite into the company's hot, fresh, yeasty doughnuts. At the dawn of the twenty-first century, Krispy Kreme doughnuts were so popular that *Fortune* magazine called them "the hottest

Vernon Carter Rudolph (1915-1973) learned how to make doughnuts from his uncle. His Krispy Kreme business grew to include 94 stores before his death. In 2005, there were more than 300 outlets in the U.S.

brand [name] in America." Incredibly, Krispy Kreme created this national sensation without doing any formal national advertising. The product sold itself.

Krispy Kreme's skyrocketing popularity in the 2000s was all the more startling given the fact that neither the company nor its product was new. Krispy Kreme has been making doughnuts since the Great Depression, but up until the late 1990s, it was only a regional operation with fewer than 100 franchises.

THE FRENCH CHEF'S RECIPE

The person who laid the groundwork for the Krispy Kreme explosion was Vernon Carver Rudolph. The oldest son of Plumie (father) and Rethie (mother) Rudolph, Vernon was born on June 30, 1915, in Marshall County, Kentucky, where Plumie ran a general store. As a boy, Vernon compiled a fine record both academically and athletically, and he also worked at the family store.

Following his high-school graduation, Vernon Rudolph went to work for his uncle Ishmael Armstrong in Paducah, Kentucky. Armstrong was the proprietor of the Krispy Kreme doughnut shop, which featured yeast doughnuts made from the recipe of Joe LeBeau, a French chef who had brought his recipe with him from New Orleans. Initially, Rudolph worked as a door-to-door salesman for his uncle's doughnuts while he learned the process of doughnut making.

During this time, the country was mired in the middle of the Great Depression and the Paducah

Doughnuts originated in the mid-1800s. They are a derivation of *olykoeken*, a treat Dutch immigrants made by frying leftover scraps of bread dough in hot oil. Olykoeken tended not to cook all the way through, so the under-cooked centers were often filled with nuts, giving them the English name "doughnuts." The hole was pioneered around 1847 when sea captain Mason Crockett Gregory poked out the centers to remove the undercooked bits.

shop began to lose money. Armstrong moved his operations to Nashville, Tennessee, in hopes that a larger population could provide the business he needed. Vernon Rudolph went with him, and they were soon joined by Rudolph's father, Plumie—whose general store had fallen victim to the bad economic times. At first, the doughnut shop seemed to be faring little better in Nashville than it had in Paducah. In 1935 Armstrong decided to call it quits, sell the shop, and move back to Kentucky. Seeing an opportunity, Vernon Rudolph wanted to buy the Krispy Kreme business from his uncle, but could not afford it. Plumie Rudolph, however, was able to obtain the money to close the deal. He bought the shop from Armstrong and ran it with Vernon and another son, Louis.

SEEKING HIS FORTUNE

The Rudolph family succeeded where Armstrong did not. In fact, the shop did so well that in 1936, Plumie Rudolph opened another in Charleston, West Virginia, followed by a third store in Atlanta. Although he was pleased that his father's venture was booming, Vernon still wanted to run a business of his own. In the summer of 1937, he decided to make his move. Rudolph loaded his new Pontiac with a few belongings and some pieces of dough-making equipment and, with no particular destination in mind, drove off to seek his fortune.

After a short time, however, Rudolph found himself in Peoria, Illinois, having gone through most of his money without finding any suitable prospects for

Most stories about Krispy Kreme's history omit mention of Armstrong and state that Vernon Rudolph bought the doughnut shop, the recipe, and the rights to the Krispy Kreme name from LeBeau. But according to the company's archives, Armstrong was the one who made the purchase from LeBeau in 1933—a more likely scenario, since Rudolph would have been only 18 at the time of the transaction.

his business. He knew he couldn't stay where he was—the rents were just too high—but he was totally at a loss about what to do and where to go next. One day, while standing on a street corner, he pulled out a pack of cigarettes and happened to notice that they were manufactured in Winston-Salem, North Carolina. "A town with a company producing a nationally advertised product has to be a good bet," he reasoned. With that, he set off driving east to the city.

By this time, Rudolph was down to his last $25. He found an affordable space to rent on Main Street in Winston-Salem, suitable for making doughnuts. Unfortunately, he had no money left for purchasing ingredients. His business plan was saved, however, when a grocer in the neighborhood agreed to lend him the ingredients on the condition that he would be repaid as soon as the first doughnuts were sold. Using the borrowed supplies and the Krispy Kreme recipe, Rudolph opened his company for business on July 13, 1937. He contented himself initially with doing business the way his family always had— selling to retail stores.

AROMA ADVERTISING

Although he never even considered marketing his doughnuts, Vernon Rudolph's product had a powerful way of advertising itself, free of charge. The aroma that wafted from his bakery had passersby drooling for a taste of his Krispy Kremes.

Originally, Rudolph had been making his deliveries out of the back seat of his Pontiac, but requests increased so rapidly that soon he had to buy trucks to deliver to stores in the area. Meanwhile, so many people stopped in asking to buy doughnuts that Rudolph finally decided to take advantage of the situation. He cut a hole in the wall of his bakery to make room for a small shop where he could sell hot, fresh doughnuts directly to customers.

The experience led Rudolph to adopt sales techniques that simply let the doughnuts work their magic on the senses. He realized the value of production windows that allowed customers to see and smell the fresh product. But Rudolph didn't just appeal to the customers' senses of sight and smell— he targeted their taste buds, too. Unwilling to sell anything that was not freshly baked, he often gave away unsold doughnuts at night rather than trying to sell them the next day. As Rudolph suspected, the taste of these free samples often brought customers back to buy hot doughnuts the next morning.

As Rudolph was establishing his business, his personal life ran a roller coaster of emotions. In 1939, he married Ruth Ayers, with whom he adopted a daughter, Patricia, in 1943. Sadly, Ruth was killed in a car accident in South Carolina in 1944. He remarried in 1946 to Lorraine Flynt, and the couple had four children together: Vernon Jr., Sanford, Curtis, and Beverly.

How the Twinkie Got Its Filling

Around the same time that Vernon Rudolph was starting out in the doughnut business, one of the most popular snack products of the twentieth century was also born—the Twinkie. Twinkies were the brainchild of Jimmy Dewar, a bakery manager in Schiller Park, Illinois. In 1930, Dewar was looking for a new, low-priced baked good that could boost business and provide his bakers with work during the difficult days of the Great Depression.

His focus fell on the pans that were used to make the cakes for strawberry shortcake. Once the strawberry season (a six-week period at the longest) was over, there was no more demand for shortcake, and the pans sat empty for the rest of the year. Dewar decided to find a use for them. On April 6, 1930, he came up with what he called "the best darn-tootin' idea I ever had." He poked a hole in the short-cake and injected it with a creamy banana filling. The inspiration for his creation's name came when Dewar was driving through St. Louis and saw a billboard advertising Twinkle Toe Shoes. Liking the sound of that, Dewar called his new product Twinkies and sold them at a price of two for a nickel. Twinkies were soon acquired by Hostess, a division of the Continental Baking Company, which also made Wonder Bread and Chocolate Cupcakes.

After its creation, there were a couple of alterations in Dewar's original Twinkie.

During World War II, most of the boats used to transport bananas to the United States from South America were commandeered for use by the U.S. Navy. With no source of bananas for the filling, the banana creme was eliminated in favor of vanilla-flavored filling. Later, the development of a completely nondairy filling eliminated the problem of early spoilage and allowed Twinkies to be shipped and sold all over the nation. Twinkies hit the West Coast in 1943 and New York in 1950.

Twinkies became a cultural icon. They inspired everything from cartoon characters to science experiments, and references to them often popped up in movies, books, and television programs. In 1999, the White House Millennium Council chose the Twinkie as "an object of enduring American symbolism" in the Nation's Millennium Time Capsule.

By 2003, the snack-cake market was a highly competitive industry, doing $900 million in business annually. The Continental Baking Company had become Interstate Bakeries Corporation, the largest independent bakery in the U.S. Its Hostess division controlled nearly 13 percent of the snack-cake market, thanks in large part to the more than 500 million Twinkies it baked every year. Other notable Hostess products included the popular Chocolate Cupcakes, Suzy Q's, Ho Hos, and Ding Dongs.

The popular Twinkie snack cake with its vanilla-flavored filling

The Krispy Kreme Company continued to use Rudolph's "aroma advertising" into the twenty-first century.

KRISPY KREME FRANCHISES

Around this same time, the growing popularity of his product prompted Rudolph to expand his enterprise. He began by starting new Krispy Kreme stores in various southeastern cities, but quickly discovered that franchising was a faster, more certain way to succeed. Instead of building and owning new stores himself, he entered into agreements with people who wished to start their own Krispy Kreme operations.

Rudolph granted them the rights to use the Krispy Kreme recipe and brand name in exchange for a fee and a promise that they would maintain the company's high standards of quality.

In 1946, Rudolph made the first of two business moves that put him in prime position to expand Krispy Kreme from a local chain into a doughnut empire. First, he consolidated all of the stores he owned into one business—the Krispy Kreme Company. The following year, he formed a separate company called the Krispy Kreme Corporation. Rudolph had discovered that he could make more money, as well as ensure quality at the same time, by manufacturing the dry doughnut mix that all Krispy Kreme franchise stores used. The corporation would be in charge of producing the dry mixes for all Krispy Kreme stores. Rudolph served as president and chairman of the board of both companies.

A couple of years later, a business setback caused Rudolph to revise his operations. In 1949, the Doughnut Corporation of America, which supplied the equipment that Krispy Kreme used in making doughnuts, announced that it was going to manufacture and sell its own doughnuts. With his supplier suddenly a major competitor, Rudolph found himself looking for a new source of equipment. He decided to turn the tables on the Doughnut Corporation of America. If his former equipment supplier was moving in on his market, he would move in on its. He now split his corporation into three divisions: the Mix Division, the Laboratory Division (where new recipes, ingredients, and products were tested), and

franchise: a licensing arrangement in which an investor pays money to the owner of a particular brand-name product or business for permission to sell that product or operate that business in a certain territory. The person offering the permission is called the **franchiser**. The person buying the rights is the **franchisee**.

the Equipment Division (which manufactured the doughnut machines that Rudolph used to buy).

Rudolph made certain that Krispy Kreme stayed current with the latest technology. During the 1950s, the company introduced a process called continuous yeast dough-making, which replaced the need to start over with a new batch of dough once the old one was used up. In 1962, he built two additional, modernized Krispy Kreme factories, one in Charlotte, North Carolina, and one in Richmond, Virginia. Rudolph also switched his stores to a revolutionary new process of doughnut manufacturing.

The company's best-selling product is the Krispy Kreme Original Glazed: a hot, glazed, raised doughnut.

Instead of being cut out by machine, the doughnuts were extruded under high pressure from the dough hopper. This process has remained in use ever since.

By the time of Vernon Rudolph's death on August 16, 1973, Krispy Kreme had grown into a large regional corporation with 94 stores. With operations modernized and streamlined, and a product that customers raved about, the company was ready to expand beyond its base in the southeastern U.S. Rudolph, however, neglected to leave any instructions as to how to distribute his wealth and run his empire after his death. The business was held in trust and run by a bank until his family found a buyer.

extrude: to push out through a die or mold

hopper: a container, typically funnel shaped, in which materials are stored before they are dispensed

STUMBLE AND RECOVERY

On May 28, 1976, Beatrice Foods, a giant conglomerate based in Chicago, bought Krispy Kreme. According to many longtime Krispy Kreme employees, the sale nearly destroyed the company. In the words of Scott Livengood, who started with Krispy Kreme in the 1970s as a human-resources trainee, "Beatrice didn't care so much if the stores made money, as long as we sold doughnuts to supermarkets. They didn't want to invest in stores or grow the company; they just wanted cash. Then they changed the logo to a tacky 70's look. And they actually messed with the doughnut formula. They made it cheaper."

The efforts of Beatrice Foods to make Krispy Kreme more profitable went nowhere, and by the early 1980s, the corporation was eager to sell the doughnut operation. A group of Krispy Kreme

The bright red and green Krispy Kreme logo

franchise owners, led by Joseph McAleer Sr., were determined to restore their company to its former prominence. They joined together to purchase Krispy Kreme back from Beatrice on February 28, 1982, for $24 million. McAleer's first move after the purchase was to restore the company's original recipe and logo.

While this helped put the company back on a solid foundation, the new group of owners encountered some obstacles that initially hindered their plans for growth. The buyers, most of whom were not wealthy individuals, had to go into considerable debt to make the purchase. This left them without the funds to expand. Even worse, the group made an agreement that any significant business decision concerning Krispy Kreme required the unanimous consent of the 21 investors—which differed from the standard business practice of requiring only a simple majority. This tended to stifle any creativity or bold actions on the company's part. As a result, the number of Krispy Kreme stores in operation dwindled substantially by 1990.

Krispy Kreme finally began to recover in the 1990s, under the leadership of a new chief executive officer, Mack McAleer (Joe's son), and Scott Livengood, who had moved up to management from the human-resources department. It was Mack who introduced "doughnut theater" as a way of enticing customers. This involved putting the entire baking process out in the open so customers could watch their fresh doughnuts actually being made and then fried. Livengood and McAleer also increased the size of their doughnuts 40 percent, made the manufacturing plant more efficient, and began to expand the company nationally.

After more than a half century of operation, Krispy Kreme finally broke out of the Southeast in 1995, when it opened a store in Indianapolis, Indiana. That move set off a chain reaction, and soon new stores were opening across the country. Krispy Kreme arrived in New York City in June 1996, and in La Habra, California, in January 1999. Two years later, Krispy Kreme went international, opening a store in Mississauga, Ontario. In virtually

Today, Krispy Kreme has rigorous standards of quality control. Everything from the raw ingredients to the finished product is sampled and tested repeatedly to ensure that a doughnut bought at the Krispy Kreme in the Excalibur Hotel in Las Vegas tastes exactly like one bought at the Krispy Kreme on 53rd Street in Davenport, Iowa. The rejected doughnuts are disposed of as pig feed.

every case, the company's arrival created a feeding frenzy—despite its lack of formal advertising.

By the late 1990s, marriages and births had increased the number of shareholders to 183. At this point, Krispy Kreme was rapidly rising in popularity, and Livengood (who had taken over in 1997 as the company's chief executive officer when Mack decided to step down) wanted to take the company public. Again, however, the need for unanimous consent among the shareholders came back to trouble the company. To offer stock for public sale, Livengood had to obtain permission to do so from each of the 183 people—a trying process that lasted years and almost failed numerous times. Eventually, however, Livengood succeeded, and Krispy Kreme was listed on the NASDAQ in April 2000. (It transferred over to the New York Stock Exchange in May 2001.) In its first year on the market, the price of the company's stock more than tripled.

LEGACY

After faltering following Vernon Rudolph's death in the 1970s, Krispy Kreme slowly got back on its feet and became one of the most remarkable success stories in the food industry in recent years. In terms of actual size, Krispy Kreme was still a rather minor figure in the sweets business—even in the doughnut business—in the early 2000s. As of September 2003, there were still only 319 Krispy Kreme outlets compared to roughly 5,700 stores worldwide (3,900 in the U.S.) for rival Dunkin' Doughnuts. But in terms of public awareness, profitability, and explosive growth,

Krispy Kreme stood unmatched. In the words of North Carolina banker Erskine Bowles, former chief of staff to President Bill Clinton, "I've never seen another company like it. It's clean, it's conservative, and I love the [profit] margins."

In 2003, Krispy Kreme was producing more than 7.5 million doughnuts a day and had stores in 41 states, Canada, and Australia, with plans in the works to open several stores in the United Kingdom. In addition to the Krispy Kreme shops, the company's products were also sold at thousands of supermarkets, convenience stores, and other retail outlets. It recorded more than $6.2 billion in system-wide sales for the 2002 fiscal year.

Krispy Kreme's sputtering history demonstrated that even a company with a superior product needs good management. It took many years for the company to be able to capitalize on customers' love of its product. The tremendous publicity buzz over Krispy Kremes suggested that the members of its management had finally found their rhythm.

But in 2005, the beat slowed for Krispy Kreme as the company's stock price dipped due to decreased sales and a federal investigation into the company's accounting practices. CEO Scott Livengood was fired and replaced by Stephen Cooper, who has earned the reputation of being an expert in restructuring companies. Of course, the product that Vernon Rudolph inherited and developed remains, and the tantalizing aroma and melt-in-the-mouth flavor of Krispy Kreme doughnuts may save the enterprise once again.

> Krispy Kreme produces enough doughnuts in one week to make a doughnut line from New York City to Los Angeles.

> November 5 is National Doughnut Day in the United States.

5

ELLEN GORDON

TOOTSIE ROLL: MAKING MILLIONS ON PENNY CANDY

The Tootsie Roll originated as the first paper-wrapped penny candy over a century ago. Today, it remains the only major brand of penny candy. It is the flagship product of a company that does nearly $400 million in business a year and has been regarded as one of the most stable, profitable companies in the United States. Many business experts, however, believe that the Tootsie Roll company would not even be in existence today were it not for the efforts of Ellen Gordon, who joined forces with her husband, Melvin, to run the company.

ON A ROLL

The Tootsie Roll was invented by Leo Hirshfield, a man with a flair for developing new food products.

As one of the first female presidents of a New York Stock Exchange-listed company, Ellen Gordon (b. 1931) was a pioneer in the business world, as well as the candy industry.

A Tootsie Roll in its orange, brown, and white paper wrapper

Among his creations was a jelling powder that was a prototype for modern gelatin products. In 1896, shortly after immigrating to Brooklyn, New York, from Austria, Hirshfield began manufacturing a solid, chewy, chocolate candy that did not easily melt. He sold these bite-sized candies, which he called Tootsie Rolls after his nickname for his daughter, Clara, for a penny each in his small store.

Tootsie Rolls were such a hit in Hirshfield's Brooklyn neighborhood that he could not keep up with the demand. Because he lacked the money to expand on his own, he merged with another local candy manufacturer, Stern and Staalberg, in 1897.

Shortly before the turn of the century, Hirshfield came up with a simple way to make his candies distinctive. At that time, all shopkeepers kept penny candy products unwrapped in glass jars or wooden barrels. Upon purchase, the candies were scooped out and bagged. Hirshfield, however, had the original idea of keeping his candy fresh and free from the contamination of handling by wrapping each piece in paper. His gamble that the appeal of this packaging would more than make up for the extra time and expense proved to be correct. The red, brown, and white wrappers Hirshfield used helped to distinguish his candy from others, and eventually they became a recognized trademark of Tootsie Rolls.

By 1905, local demand for Tootsie Rolls was so great that Hirshfield moved into a four-story factory in New York City. In 1917, he made the decision to market his products nationwide and called his business Sweets Company of America. Ever expanding in sales and revenue, Hirshfield's company stock was traded on the New York Stock Exchange, starting in 1922.

BEGINNINGS OF A DYNASTY

In 1931, several significant events impacted the course of Tootsie Roll's history. First, despite the brutal economic conditions of the Great Depression, the company introduced a successful new product, the Tootsie Pop, which was basically a Tootsie Roll inside a lollipop.

The original Tootsie Roll factory. Tootsie Rolls were made in this New York plant until 1938.

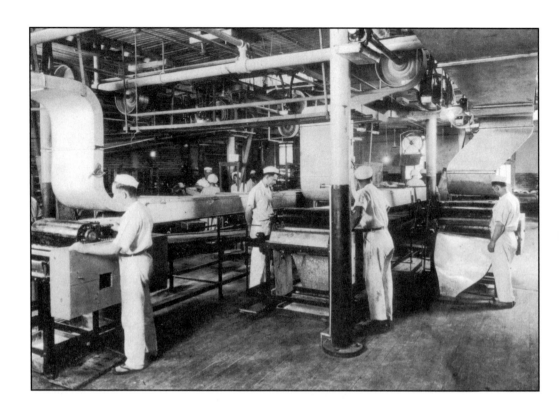

The Sweets Company of America in about 1920

Next, William Rubin, who ran the paper-manufacturing company that supplied packaging material for Hirshfield, took an interest in the Sweets Company of America. His wife, a schoolteacher, had been making an excellent return from the shares of stock she had purchased in the company. Rubin noticed that this profitable company often had trouble paying its bills. Suspecting that a quality product was being hampered by weak management, he quietly began buying shares—with the goal of eventually taking control of the company. Also in 1931, the Rubins' daughter, Ellen, was born in New York City.

As William accumulated shares of stock, the Sweets Company of America continued to flourish. It fared particularly well during World War II, when Tootsie Rolls' ability to hold up to severe weather conditions made the candy an appealing choice for soldiers' rations. In the meantime, Ellen grew up in a privileged world with a comfortable home and an education in top private schools. She was particularly adept at math and seemed to have a keen head for business. Her father would often come home and talk business with her or take her along with him to the office, where she sometimes occupied her time by adding up phone numbers in the directory.

Many products, including sugar, were rationed or limited during World War II. This forced most of the companies in the confectionery industry to reduce or suspend production. Tootsie Rolls, however, were packed in soldiers' rations because the candy had a long shelf life, as well as being a good source of quick energy. As a result, the company thrived during a difficult time.

WHEN   THE   BOYS   COME   HOME

Tootsie Rolls

THE GREATEST DESERVE
THE BEST

THE SWEETS COMPANY
OF AMERICA, NEW YORK

A big part of Tootsie Roll's success was its popularity with American troops who served in both world wars. This ad celebrated the return home of soldiers after World War I.

By 1948, Ellen had finished high school and was trying to decide what to do with her life. At that time, girls were discouraged from going into business or studying math. During her senior year she had written a paper in which she declared that her goal was to become a businesswoman. But she concluded the paper by writing, "Of course, this is just a joke. I'm going to get married and have children and be very happy to do that." She remembers everyone thinking her essay was very humorous. Even her father, although he recognized her business gifts, wanted her to get married, stay home, and raise a family. But math continued to intrigue her and when she attended Vassar College, she entered as one of the few math majors on campus.

Also by 1948, William Rubin had accumulated enough stock to take over the Sweets Company of America. One of the first decisions he made as president of the company was to put more effort into advertising. To this end, he put his daughter to work. In 1950, he took out a full-page ad in *Life* magazine. The picture showed an 18-year-old Ellen Rubin smiling alongside Tootsie Roll products and surrounded by the words "Sweet! Popular! Wholesome!"

William Rubin did not concentrate solely on print advertisements, however. His company was also one of the first to take out extensive ads in the new medium of television, particularly on programs that were aimed at children, such as *The Howdy Doody Show* and the *Mickey Mouse Club*.

The 1950 Life *magazine ad featuring 18-year-old Ellen Gordon*

JUGGLING MOTHERHOOD AND CAREER

Around the same time the ad in *Life* appeared, Ellen, by then a sophomore at Vassar, met Melvin Gordon, a former football player for Harvard University who had become a successful textile executive. Despite a 12-year age gap between the two, they fell in love and were married before the year was out.

Saving Life Savers

For years, one of Tootsie Roll's main rivals in the lollipop and hard candy arena was Life Savers, a candy with a history almost as long as that of Tootsie Roll.

Shortly after the turn of the twentieth century, Clarence Crane was a Cleveland confectioner concentrating on chocolates. In the summer of 1912, however, he became frustrated by the way his candies would melt into gooey lumps when the weather got hot, and he decided to try something new. After weighing his options, Crane settled on making mints. He did not have any machinery suitable for making hard candies, so he hired a pill manufacturer to produce his new product. Unlike traditional mints, most of which had pillow-like shapes, Crane's candies were punched out in small circles, thus inspiring their name—Life Savers.

Although Crane's new candy had a novel shape, customers were not particularly interested in his Pep-O-Mint Life Savers. The mints had difficulty catching on because their flavor had a short shelf life—often by the time a customer had purchased a roll, the candies had lost their taste. When Crane received an offer from New York businessman Edward Noble to buy the Life Savers' recipe, trademark, and production rights, he sold the struggling brand for $2,900.

Noble discovered that the reason Life Savers lost their flavor so quickly was because of their cardboard containers. The tubes weren't airtight enough to preserve freshness for extended periods. To remedy this problem, he developed tinfoil packaging to keep the candy flavorful longer. Noble then came up with an imaginative and energetic sales campaign to generate interest in Life Savers candies. These two business moves greatly increased sales. In 1935, now with a steady income, the company was able to introduce the five-fruit-flavor roll that became its best seller.

Except for replacing three of the original flavors with new ones in 2003, Life Savers candy remained virtually unchanged for almost 70 years. As of 2005, Life Savers were produced at the rate of about 100 rolls per minute, with 125 million individual candies eaten every day.

Life Savers changed its classic five-flavor roll in 2003. Raspberry, watermelon, and blackberry flavors replaced the traditional orange, lemon, and lime "O's." Pineapple and cherry flavors remained in the new roll.

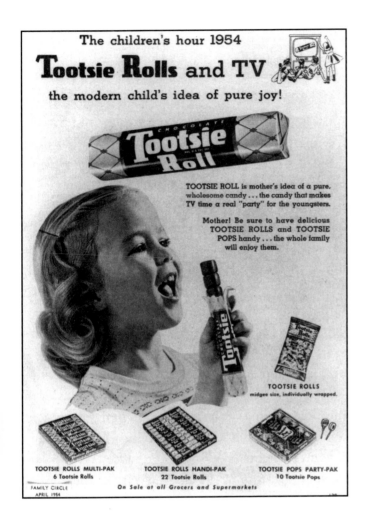

This print ad ran concurrently with Tootsie Roll's groundbreaking television advertisements on popular children's shows.

After the wedding, Ellen transferred to Wellesley
College in Boston, where one of Melvin's offices was
located. Before she could complete her degree, however, she became pregnant. At that time, it was
uncommon for women who had or were starting
families to attend college. Telling her it was
"unseemly . . . to be in a family way [pregnant]"
while in college, both faculty and family members

Tootsie Roll moved to its Chicago factory in 1966. This central location allowed goods to be shipped more economically across the U.S. It also made corn syrup, a staple product of many regional refineries, easier to obtain.

strongly pressured her to leave school. She did and spent the rest of the 1950s at home raising her first two children.

In 1962, Melvin Gordon was named Rubin's successor as chief executive officer of the Sweets Company of America. By that time, Ellen had decided she could be both a mother and a student. Following the birth of her third child, she enrolled at Brandeis University. She spent much of her time juggling her studies, taking her third daughter to nursery school, and taking care of the other two at home. After finally obtaining her college degree in 1965, she moved on to graduate school at Harvard University, where she studied Indo-European linguistics. She cut short these studies in 1968, however, when Melvin asked her to join the company—now renamed Tootsie Roll Industries—as a director.

Melvin had come to appreciate Ellen's savvy in the field of investments, and her first assignment was to manage the company's pension fund and outside investments. Although corporate takeovers by outside investors were relatively rare in those days, Ellen was concerned that Tootsie Roll stockholders might be tempted to make a quick profit by selling their shares to another company, which would then control Tootsie Roll. To prevent this, she made it a top priority to invest in such a way that her family increased the percentage of company stock it owned. As long as the family owned more than 50 percent of voting shares, she knew that Tootsie Roll Industries could not be sold without their consent.

Jelly Bellys: Full of Flavors and Success

The jellybean, like Tootsie Rolls, a sweet and chewy confection, traces its history back to a candy known as Turkish delight—a jellied treat that has been around since Biblical times.

The candy coating that surrounds the gummy center, however, didn't emerge until the late nineteenth century. At that time, penny candies were rapidly gaining popularity, and confectioners began to experiment with new forms of jellied treats in an attempt to take advantage of this trend. Perhaps the most well-received concoction was one in which the candy was molded into the shape of a large bean and given a hard, sugary shell that kept the candies from sticking together. No one is sure precisely when (or even by whom) the modern jellybean was invented, but advertisements have been discovered from as early as 1861 urging the public to send jellybeans to soldiers fighting in the Civil War.

One of the most well-known jellybean manufacturers is the Jelly Belly Candy Company. Originally called the Herman Goelitz Candy Co., it was founded in Belleville, Illinois, by brothers Gustav and Albert Goelitz. In 1869, only a few years after immigrating to the U.S. from Germany, the two men began making and selling ice cream and hard candies. Around 1900, their children took over the company and expanded the product line to include such candies as butter creams, candy corn, and jellybeans. Eventually, the company's jellybeans became so well known that Goelitz Candy switched its name to the more whimsical Jelly Belly. As with other manufacturers of jellybeans, the company sold a few standard flavors mixed together in bags.

In the 1970s, a candy distributor in Los Angeles approached the company with a suggestion that it make naturally flavored jellybeans. Jelly Belly liked the idea, and in 1976 it introduced its first eight new flavors (Very Cherry, Lemon, Grape, Creme Soda, Tangerine, Licorice, Root Beer, and Green Apple). The products were sold in mixed bags, as well as being sold separately according to flavor.

Jelly Bellys received a huge publicity boost in the early 1980s, when it was discovered that President-elect Ronald Reagan had a great fondness for them. As a result, three tons of red, white, and blue Jelly Bellys (blueberry was a new flavor made just for Reagan) were provided for his inauguration in 1981.

By 2003, the company (now based in Fairfield, California) offered 50 flavors of jellybeans, the most popular of which were Very Cherry and Buttered Popcorn. In addition to its beans, Jelly Belly also made more than 100 other popular confections, including Jordan Almonds, Candy Corn, and Gummi Bears.

A RAPID RISE

Ellen Gordon had only been on the job about a year when she became pregnant with her fourth daughter. This time, rather than step down, she was determined to handle business and family life together. In doing so, she became something of a pioneer. Few companies had any high-ranking female executives at all, much less one who was a mother of a young child.

Because of her unique situation, Gordon often had to deal with workplace prejudice. On one occasion, for example, she was supposed to lead an important meeting that had been scheduled to be held at an all-men's club. Management, however, refused to allow her in the building. Finally, her coworkers sneaked her in through a back entryway.

Being a working mother meant Gordon sometimes had to be creative in her scheduling. In order to spend time with her youngest daughter, she took her along on business trips to Chicago, where the company had relocated in 1966. "I once nursed my baby at the stock exchange and thought they'd throw me out," she recalled. "They didn't know what to do with me. But I held my ground."

Ellen Gordon did so well at her job that she rapidly moved up in the company. When asked about her work ethic, Melvin called her the most persistent person he had ever seen in business. "She will go over, around, under, or through a problem, but she won't stop until she has the answer," he said. In 1972 Ellen's relentless telephone pursuit of possible

"I can remember the days when I had to go in the back door to a board of directors' meeting because they weren't allowing women in the front door."
—Ellen Gordon

business acquisitions for the company helped pave the way for Tootsie Roll's purchase of Mason Dots and Bonomo Turkish Taffy. Soon, she was promoted to corporate secretary, then to vice president in charge of product development in 1974, and finally to senior vice president in 1977. A year later, in an attempt to revitalize the company's sales, Ellen Gordon was named president and chief operating officer of Tootsie Roll Industries. This promotion made her only the second woman to be president of a company listed on the New York Stock Exchange. For more than a quarter-century, she would continue to run Tootsie Roll Industries in cooperation with Melvin, who served as the company's chief executive officer.

COOPERATIVE MANAGEMENT

The Gordons' management of Tootsie Roll was a cooperative venture unique in the history of corporate America. Ellen and Melvin, who worked in offices that faced each other, were committed to working as a team. They made a point of discussing whatever business issues came up, and they tried to explore those issues from every possible point of view. When they disagreed on matters, their policy was to never undertake any action unless one of them could convince the other that it was the right thing to do.

Ellen Gordon discovered early in her career that raising four children provided valuable insight in managing a large company. "It makes you very efficient with time," she said. "You've got to send them off to school and your husband to work. It's like an executive. You're directing people."

Gordon believed that one of the keys to managing a large company was recognizing that the top person did not have to know all the answers or make all the decisions. She constantly sought input and innovations from her employees, who knew more about the specific details of their jobs than she did. She described her management style as a reflection of the patient yet firm manner needed to keep a household running. While Gordon could be aggressive when needed, she tended to do so in a quiet, persuasive way, rather than being loud and angry or trying to show that she was tough.

STRATEGIC FOCUS

Ellen Gordon's leadership at Tootsie Roll focused on three areas: growth through acquisitions, staying out of debt, and production efficiency. She realized early that in order to survive against the giants of the candy industry, Hershey and Mars, Tootsie Roll would have to keep growing. But she also recognized the difficulty of trying to increase sales by adding new products. Sweets consumers are notoriously loyal to long-established brands that they have eaten since childhood, and the vast majority of new products in the industry fail quickly. Gordon also knew that there was limited room for growth with the company's established products, Tootsie Pops and Tootsie Rolls. The solution for her was to buy small companies that had been in business for a long

Tootsie Roll had a number of clever and catchy campaigns featuring advertisements such as the one shown here.

time and made unique products that had found a loyal following.

Under Gordon's direction, Tootsie Roll began buying out these companies in 1985, starting with the purchase of Cellas' Confections, makers of chocolate-covered cherries. The company took an even bolder step in 1988 with the acquisition of the Charms Company for $65 million. This made Tootsie Roll the world's largest producer of lollipops.

In 1993, Gordon pulled off one of the biggest deals in the company's history: the $81-million purchase of the chocolate and caramel brands that belonged to Warner-Lambert Company, including Sugar Daddy, Sugar Babies, Charleston Chew, and Junior Mints. According to one industry analyst, Gordon's strategy was to acquire established businesses with strong followings and then "add snap and pizzazz to the companies they buy."

Junior & Dot Together At Last!

Tootsie Roll was careful to make these purchases without going into debt, a policy that Gordon attributed to her upbringing. Her parents, who struggled during the Great Depression of the 1930s, drove home to her the dangers that could result from taking on debt. Gordon also tried to hold business costs lower by keeping most operations in-house rather than hiring outside people. Tootsie Roll constructed its own sugar refinery, created its own advertising agency, and even built printing presses to make its own candy wrappers.

The final element of Gordon's leadership focus was lowering costs of production through automation. When she took over the company, she discovered the factories were using outdated and inefficient machinery. "Making candy is not a high-margin business," she noted, "so we have to run a very lean operation." To her, that meant spending money up front to save money in the long run. In 1983, Gordon initiated a $10 million modernization program that allowed the factories to make much more candy at far less cost. Five years later, she oversaw a similar massive overhaul of the company's office computers.

LEGACY

The result of Gordon's efforts was a remarkable run of success. According to industry analyst David Leibowitz, "Tootsie Roll had lost its way before she came on board as president. Under her watch, the company has been on quite a tear and the numbers have improved tremendously." Tootsie Roll's sales tripled between 1979 and 1991. Although Gordon was criticized in later years when the company's sales growth began to slow slightly, Tootsie Roll soon perked back up and remained one of the nation's largest candy manufacturers. In 2002, the company did $393 million worth of business and produced more than 60 million Tootsie Rolls and 20 million Tootsie Pops per day. Although it had a small share of the overall market when compared to giants like Hershey and Mars, Tootsie Roll clearly dominated the non-chocolate and lollipop segments of the candy industry, with a more than 50 percent share.

Ellen Gordon also stood as a role model among women executives. In May 1984, she became the first woman to win the candy industry's Kettle Award for outstanding leadership in the business. In 1995, the George Washington University School of Business named her its CEO of the year.

When she first took over the presidency at Tootsie Roll, Ellen Gordon thought she was alone in the business world. In 1982, after discovering other female executives scattered throughout the ranks of U.S. business, she helped found the Committee of 200, an organization devoted to supporting women in business. *Working Woman* magazine called Gordon "an executive who has used her skills as a business person, rather than relied on her role as a 'woman president.'" This description is one she hopes can be applied to all industry professionals. "I hope the day comes when we think of management style being related to individuals, not their gender," Gordon said.

In 2003, Tootsie Roll remained a profitable multimillion-dollar company. Even after more than a century in business, it continued to thrive in the cut-throat world of confections. Experts agree that Gordon's early commitment to keeping the company's stock shares in the control of her family saved the company from being swallowed up by another giant corporation. With control of as much as 70 percent of the voting shares, the Gordons were able to keep the company independent. That control also allowed them to focus on the long-term needs of the company. As Gordon explained in 2000, "We are not interested in any immediate return that might affect our ability to be around for the next 103 years."

Melvin and Ellen Gordon. "We're stronger as a couple than we would be as two individuals," said Melvin Gordon.

6

WALLY AMOS

THE COOKIE MANAGER

Wally Amos spent a good portion of his career as one of the first African American talent agents and managers. Working in the field of popular music, Amos was the agent who recognized the talents of such singers as the Supremes and Paul Simon and Art Garfunkel. But his most successful client was not a singer or an entertainer—it wasn't even a living being. Amos made his fortune and national reputation by promoting a cookie just as if it were one of his entertainment clients. His Famous Amos chocolate chip cookies took the nation by storm in the mid-1970s and have retained a faithful following ever since.

THE EARLY YEARS

Wallace Amos Jr. was born in Tallahassee, Florida, on July 1, 1936. His parents, Wallace and Ruby

"The face that launched a thousand chips" belonged to Wallace Amos Jr. (b. 1936, left), pictured here with his son, Gregory, at a book signing.

Amos, were both uneducated people who had to work hard at their unskilled labor jobs to make ends meet (Wallace at a local gas plant and Ruby as a household servant). As a result they were seldom home. Nonetheless, they were able to provide their son with such a strict, religious upbringing that young Wally believed he was destined to become a preacher.

At first, Wally had to walk four miles to Lincoln School, a combination high school and elementary school for blacks. Dissatisfied with the poor facilities and quality of education, his parents eventually enrolled him in a new, smaller school at their church. When he was not in school, Wally was able to earn money by delivering newspapers and starting his own shoeshine business.

In 1948, Wallace and Ruby separated. Wally initially moved with his mother to Orlando, Florida. After a month, however, he moved to New York City to live with his Aunt Della and Uncle Fred, whom he had visited during the past two summers. Wally's mother encouraged him to make the move, believing that opportunities for a young black man were greater in the North than in Florida. This did, indeed, turn out to be the case. For example, in New York, Amos experienced a racially integrated learning situation for the first time while attending Edwin Stitt Junior High School.

Della ran a much more joyful household than Amos had experienced with his parents. Frequently, she baked delicious chocolate-chip cookies, and Wally never forgot the cheerful banter that accompanied

"All Aunt Della needed to see was me with a sad face, and *boom*! Into the kitchen for cookies."
—Wally Amos

those efforts. Della explained that, for best results, you had to talk nicely to the cookies and turn them often while they were baking.

Happy as he was sharing a room with his cousin Joe, Wally nearly gave it up to return to Tallahassee to live with his father. While Wally was visiting Florida, Wallace Sr. had promised him a new motor scooter if he would stay. Wally was ready to agree when his mother intervened, warning him that if he did not return to New York she would come to Tallahassee and drag him back. Shortly thereafter, Ruby herself moved to New York and found a small

Years later, Wally Amos revisited his childhood home in Florida. He was photographed among old washtubs in the backyard.

place in Harlem for the two of them. In the end, Wally had it to himself most of the time, as Ruby was hardly ever there after she found a good-paying job as a live-in maid for a family on Long Island.

SEARCHING FOR A CAREER

In 1951, Wally had to make a decision about which high school to attend. He selected the Food Trades Vocational High School in New York City after one of its recruiters told him that cooks could earn high wages. By the time he was 17, however, Wally had grown discouraged over the the lack of opportunities he was being given. Although the treatment of blacks was better up north than it was in the South, conditions were still less than ideal.

In 1953, Wally joined the Air Force, where he was able to complete his high school degree while serving in the armed forces. The experience gave him a chance to travel as well, and he served on bases in New York, Mississippi, Hawaii, and California. It also helped teach him some accountability for his actions when he drew two courts-martial for breaking rules about drinking and gambling.

Upon fulfilling his service obligation in 1957, Amos returned to New York and went back to school. While attending the College Secretarial Institute, he found a job as a stock clerk at the upscale Saks Fifth Avenue department store. In 1958, he married Maria LaForey, with whom he had a son, Michael. Soon, Amos's hard work and initiative on the job impressed his bosses enough to earn him a promotion to supply-department manager. It appeared Amos and his family had settled into a stable lifestyle.

In 1961, when Maria was pregnant with their second son, Amos suddenly left Saks after a salary disagreement. During the search for a new job, he got a call from one of his contacts at the Secretarial Institute, who was able to arrange an interview for him at the William Morris Talent Agency. Amos found himself in the right place at the right time. Although he had no particular training or experience, he interviewed at a time when William Morris was taking severe criticism for representing many black entertainers but hiring no black agents. Amos showed enough potential for the business that he was hired in 1961 as a mail-room secretary for a newly formed department responsible for representing performers in rock music.

AMOS THE AGENT

Amos was dedicated to doing his job well, and soon he worked his way up to secretary, then assistant agent, and finally agent. The first performers he signed at William Morris were a pair of scruffy club singers who no one else in the agency wanted to represent: Simon and Garfunkel. In 1964, Amos showed similar foresight in booking the Supremes for a Dick Clark tour.

Amos's extreme devotion to his career led to problems at home, and he and Maria divorced in 1962. He remarried five years later to singer Shirlee Ellis; the couple had a son the following year. Around the same time, Amos became disillusioned

"I [started] as a messenger in the William Morris mailroom. . . . I'd gone from being the manager of the supply department at Saks, earning $85 a week, to mailroom gofer taking a $35 a week pay cut. But, sometimes you have to set your ego aside to accomplish your long-term objectives."
—Wally Amos

Wally Amos has three sons: Michael, Gregory, and Shawn.

with his career at William Morris. "We had entered the hard rock, or acid and psychedelic rock, phase of music," he said, "and I was having difficulty relating to the loudness." Plus, after more than six years with the company, he did not feel he was advancing anywhere. Amos had been denied promotions to the film and TV departments; he was not given the chance to head the music division either.

In 1967, searching for a fresh start in life, Amos left William Morris to begin managing his own clients. He placed much of his hope in a talented South African jazz trumpeter named Hugh Masakela. Amos moved to Los Angeles in an effort to advance Masakela's career, only to have his client jump to a different manager. Despite this setback, Amos continued to work as a personal manager, finding bookings for clients on television talk shows, then managing acts for Venture Records.

REDISCOVERING COOKIES

In 1970, Amos tasted some chocolate-chip cookies made from a recipe on the back of a package of chocolate chips that reminded him of his Aunt Della's. Using a version of the recipe, he began baking his own cookies, and before long he was using the tasty treats as a promotional tool to create goodwill among producers and industry executives. Amos found that they came in quite handy in helping potential clients remember the artist-management firm of Wally Amos and Company. He bagged his cookies and brought them to meetings and television and motion-picture sets, where he passed them out freely.

Although Amos continued to struggle in his efforts to develop a stable roster of clients, the cookies were a hit. "It reached a point where people wouldn't say 'hello' when they saw me," he recalled. "They'd say 'where are my cookies?' Everybody told me I should go into the cookie business, but I didn't take the idea seriously at the time."

For years Amos hovered on the edge of success, promoting actors who dumped him for new managers, and comics and singers whose careers never took off. By October 1974, he had grown so discouraged that he thought of getting out of the business—but he had no idea what to do instead. One day, on a visit to a recording studio, he brought his trademark batch of cookies. A secretary at the company, B. J. Gilmore, commented that his cookies were exceptionally good. She suggested that they go into business together selling his chocolate chip cookies.

INTRODUCING "THE COOKIE"

Amos had heard such comments before, but this time he decided to take them seriously and actually open a store. Despite his mediocre success in recent years, there were plenty of people in Hollywood who were familiar with him and his cookies. Those contacts could be useful in two ways. First, he might be able to persuade some of the wealthy contacts to invest a little of their money in his venture to get it started. Second, he knew the value of star power in

Toll House: The Original Chocolate Chip

Wally Amos was on to something when he started his company—cookies are the most popular dessert in the United States, and chocolate chip is the most popular flavor. More than half of all home-baked cookies are chocolate chip, and many of them are made from the same recipe Amos based his cookies on—the Nestlé Toll House recipe.

The Nestlé recipe is not only a favorite of cookie fans, but it is also the original chocolate-chip recipe. As common as they are today, chocolate-chip cookies weren't even invented until the 1930s. The woman responsible for this delicious culinary concoction was Ruth Graves Wakefield. In 1930, Ruth and her husband opened the Toll House Inn. Located between Boston and New Bedford, Massachusetts, the Cape Cod-style bed-and-breakfast quickly became known for its

incredible menus. Wakefield took traditional Colonial recipes and modified them to suit more modern tastes. Her specialty was desserts, and people came from all over New England to sample them.

One day while preparing cookies, Wakefield discovered she did not have as much baker's chocolate as she needed for a particular chocolate cookie. After searching the inn's storehouse, she found some semisweet chocolate bars that Andrew Nestlé, of the Nestlé company, had given her. Wakefield cut up the bars into tiny pieces and added them to the cookie batter. She thought that when the cookies baked, the chocolate would melt and flavor them. Much to her surprise, the chocolate pieces held their shape during

baking. Wakefield's guests loved this new treat, however, and the chocolate-chip cookie was born.

The cookies grew in popularity, and Wakefield's recipe was published in numerous New England newspapers. Nestlé saw an increase in sales of its semi-sweet chocolate bar and offered to print Ruth Wakefield's "Toll House" cookie recipe on the back of the bar's packaging. In exchange for printing the popular recipe, Nestlé provided Wakefield with an unlimited supply of chocolate for the rest of her life. Eventually, the company began selling its chocolate in bite-sized pieces to help make baking the cookies easier (since the customers would no longer have to break up the bar themselves). Called Nestlé Toll House Real Semi-Sweet Chocolate Morsels since 1939, the product still had Wakefield's recipe printed on it in the twenty-first century.

After creating the chocolate-chip cookie, Ruth Wakefield continued her culinary inventions at the Toll House Inn until 1966, and she also authored a series of popular cookbooks. Wakefield died in 1977.

Hollywood. If he could get his cookies connected in the public mind to the fashionable crowd of celebrities, he could generate free publicity for himself. After Amos went around town pitching his idea to potential investors—with batches of cookies attached to the business proposal—he was able to attract start-up money from such entertainers as singers Helen Reddy and Marvin Gaye, in addition to bank loans.

In March 1975, Amos opened up his store, which he called Famous Amos Cookies. As he thought about how to ensure success for his risky new venture, Amos realized that his career as a professional manager could prove useful. The key to success for his business, as he saw it, was to use the media to turn his cookies into celebrities. "I manage The Cookie," he once observed. "I'm doing the same things for its career that I'd do for any artist."

A month before his store opened for business, Amos flooded the local media with flashy announcements of its arrival on the corner of Sunset Boulevard and Formosa Avenue. "The Cookies Are Coming!" blared his ads. He prepared a special biography of The Cookie just as he would for an entertainment client, and even gained permission from William Morris and a record company in town to use their logos in the ads, as if the cookies were a real performer. Even Los Angeles mayor Tom Bradley aided Amos's drive for publicity by declaring the store's opening day, March 9, 1975, as "Chocolate Chip Cookie Day."

THE "CELEBRITY" COOKIE

The day before the opening, Amos was up all night baking cookies. He was careful not to cut corners on ingredients. He realized that all the hype in the world would not sustain sales if his "celebrity" cookies turned out to be nothing more than ordinary, run-of-the-mill cookies.

Amos took advantage of the initial rush of interest in his product on opening day, and he continued to find ways to gain attention for his cookies. He was always available for interviews for television news stories and magazine articles. Taking a cue from his aunt, he spoke of the need to talk to the cookies while they were baking—to give them words of encouragement so they would turn out best. He began calling them "gourmet cookies" in order to appeal to those who wanted to eat only the best-quality snack food. With his colorful personality,

"People talk about good timing. But good timing can only be seen in hindsight. When I started Famous Amos, the price of sugar was at an all-time high, margarine was high, and economic conditions were bad, so they said. I did not allow the naysayers to stop me. I went ahead and planted the seeds, and the results are now history."
—Wally Amos

Amos soon became as famous as the cookies he produced. His own growing celebrity status was aided
by the photograph of himself, front and center, on
the cookie packaging.

Despite the generous flood of publicity, nothing
came easily to Amos that first year. He worked long
hours and barely made enough money to cover his
bills, let alone pay his own salary. But as his carefully
orchestrated media blitz spread from Los Angeles,
there grew more demand for the cookies than he

Wally Amos sits in front of his first store on opening day. "When I started the Famous Amos Cookie Company," he said, "people told me I couldn't start a business that sold only chocolate-chip cookies . . . because it had never been done before. I told them, 'It's time somebody did, and that somebody is me.'"

Wally Amos's smiling face graced all of the cookie packages and other company displays, even this delivery van.

could fulfill. When he received a call from a Macy's store in San Francisco inquiring about the availability of the treats, Amos decided to expand from a simple store to a wholesale cookie baker. That strategy proved hugely successful. In his second year of operations, Amos signed a contract with the prestigious Bloomingdale's store of New York to provide gourmet cookies, a move that won him thousands of fans on the East Coast. Even better, this arrangement allowed him to enter a float in Macy's Thanksgiving Day parade, thus introducing 20 million television viewers around the country to Famous Amos Cookies.

THE COOKIE CRUMBLES

Famous Amos Cookies became one of the most spectacular success stories in the food industry. By the early 1980s, Wally Amos had accumulated a personal fortune of more than $80 million. Millions of Americans recognized his brand-name, gourmet cookies with their trademark logo of a bearded Famous Amos smiling and wearing a white Panama hat. In 1977, Amos (who had been divorced from Shirlee since 1972) moved to Hawaii with his third

Wally Amos (lower left) and The Cookie made the cover of Time *magazine in 1977.*

wife, Christine. While there and enjoying the fruits of his labors, he signed on as a spokesperson for Literacy Volunteers of America (LVA). This organization was founded as a network of local, state, and regional groups that offer free one-on-one or small-group tutoring to adults who want to learn to read.

Amos's cookie enterprise, however, flamed out as spectacularly as it had arisen. As he later admitted, "My greatest downfall when I started Famous Amos was thinking I knew everything myself. I didn't and I lost my company, my millions, and my name." By 1985, Famous Amos Cookies was rapidly losing money. In an attempt to save his business, Amos began selling parts of it off to outside investors. Little by little, his share of the company dwindled. After the first sale in 1985, he was reduced to 17 percent ownership. A year later, he was left with zero percent. Now, his only role in the company he founded was simply to act as a spokesperson and promote and publicize the company. In 1988, frustrated by his limited role, he left Famous Amos altogether.

In 1991, after two years of concentrating on his volunteer work, Amos decided to get back into the cookie business. He started a company called "Wally Amos Presents: Chip & Cookie," and began promotions immediately. Unfortunately, he made a serious mistake by not researching the legalities of the Famous Amos name. It turned out that his old company still owned the rights to it. In the series of lawsuits began by Famous Amos Cookies in 1992, Wally Amos lost the right to use his own name in his business dealings.

"Living in the wake of losing Famous Amos has been a very positive experience for me, even though you may not see it on paper. . . . I am much stronger now because I have the wisdom of my experience."
—Wally Amos

STARTING OVER

Forced to start over, but undaunted, Amos changed the name of his cookie line to "Uncle Noname" and opened for business in Hawaii. When it became clear the cookie market was too crowded for any sort of success given his limited resources, he changed the company's name to "Uncle Wally's" and began marketing gourmet, fat-free muffins. In the meantime, he continued his volunteer work with LVA and made public speaking appearances throughout the country.

In 1999, the Keebler Cookie Company bought Famous Amos Cookies. After the acquisition, Keebler offered Amos the opportunity to again represent the cookies that he had popularized initially.

Wally Amos (center) appeared with boxing champion Muhammad Ali. Amos's wife, Christine, was by his side.

Wally Amos and his wife, Christine, at the Smithsonian Institute in 1980. Amos donated his trademark Hawaiian shirt and Panama hat to the Smithsonian's Business Americana Collection.

Wally Amos was once more "managing The Cookie." In 2000, able to use his own name again, Amos also relaunched his "Chip & Cookie" line of cookies.

LEGACY

For nearly a decade and a half, Wally Amos had to stand on the sidelines while the Famous Amos cookies that he had created prospered and made money for others. But that disaster both educated and inspired him. Instead of bemoaning his fate, he remained positive and began to write about his experiences and what they taught him about life. Starting in the mid-1990s, Amos turned out a series of popular philosophy books including *The Power in You: Ten Secret Ingredients for Inner Strength*; *Man With No Name: Turning Lemons into Lemonade*; *Watermelon Magic: Seeds of Wisdom, Slices of Life*; and *The Cookie Never Crumbles: Inspirational Recipes for Everyday Living*.

Wally Amos demonstrated, with astonishing force, the power of product identity. He was an amateur cookie baker who brought little product expertise to his business. Basically, he sold a version of a cookie whose recipe had been available to home bakers for generations. Through skillful use of marketing, management, and business connections, he created an identity for his product as a gourmet, or "celebrity," cookie.

Although he lost his first company because of his business inexperience, Wally Amos still made an impact on the snack-food market. Famous Amos remained a popular national brand of cookie into the twenty-first century, and it spawned a host of similar products touting their use of premium ingredients. Amos's Uncle Wally's Wholesome Baked Goods also continued to thrive. In 2001, the company opened a 43,000-square-foot bakery, and in 2002 its sales were almost $20 million. By 2003, it had become the number-one brand of store-bought muffins.

7

BEN COHEN AND JERRY GREENFIELD

GOOD WILL, GOOD TIMES, GOOD ICE CREAM

The rise of Ben & Jerry's ice cream has been one of the most interesting success stories in the business world. When Ben Cohen and Jerry Greenfield decided to open an ice-cream shop, neither one of them had any experience in running a business—Cohen was an arts and crafts teacher; Greenfield was a laboratory technician. Unlike most aspiring entrepreneurs, they sought a peaceful lifestyle in a small college community rather than the bustle of commerce centers. According to Greenfield, they went into the ice-cream trade simply because "we wanted to do something that would be more fun." Both, in fact, were so suspicious of the corporate

Jerry Greenfield (b. 1951) and Ben Cohen (b. 1951, right) scoop ice cream at a 1998 Free Cone Day promotion in one of their franchise shops.

world that they considered bailing out of the whole enterprise when the company outgrew its homey facilities in Burlington, Vermont.

Instead of folding up shop or conforming to standard business practices, however, they decided to rewrite the rules of how a corporation should be run. As a result, Ben & Jerry's became known not only for making some of the richest, most exotic ice cream on the market, but also for being one of the most innovative, freewheeling, community-minded, and socially conscious companies in the world.

CHILDHOOD FRIENDS

Jerry Greenfield and Bennett Cohen were born just four days apart in 1951, both in Brooklyn, New York, to comfortable, middle-class families. Greenfield's father worked as a stockbroker; Cohen's father was an accountant. Both boys grew up in Merrick, Long Island, and they first met during seventh-grade gym class at the public junior high. "We were the two slowest, chubbiest guys in the seventh grade," recalled Greenfield. Their common struggles forged a permanent bond of friendship between them. They remained close friends at Calhoun High School in Merrick, going on double dates together in Cohen's Camaro convertible.

Greenfield was an excellent student who set his sights on a medical career. Following high school, he enrolled at Oberlin College in Ohio, with an emphasis on pre-med courses. Upon graduation, however, he was rejected by the medical schools to which he applied.

Greenfield's favorite class at Oberlin was Carnival Techniques. In it, he learned such useful skills as how to swallow fire and how to break cinderblocks on someone's stomach with a sledgehammer. The tricks proved useful later in life when he and Cohen, (dressed up as Habeeni-Ben-Coheeni), would perform at Ben & Jerry's sponsored events.

Meanwhile, Cohen worked part-time driving an ice-cream van, and eventually he was promoted to being a product distributor for other drivers. He attended Colgate University in New York for a year and a half, but then dropped out and resumed working for the ice-cream company. Cohen tried the college scene again, briefly, this time at Skidmore College in Saratoga Springs, New York, where he became interested in pottery. After leaving Skidmore, he returned to New York City and continued studying ceramics while working a variety of part-time jobs including taxi driver, delivery person, and hospital emergency-room clerk. He eventually found part-time positions as an arts and crafts therapist at Jacobi Hospital in the Bronx, and at the Grand Street Settlement House in Manhattan.

THE LURE OF THE MOUNTAINS

While living in New York, Ben Cohen linked up again with his old friend Jerry Greenfield and shared his apartment with him. Greenfield, who was working as a laboratory technician, still harbored dreams of medical school. But after his second round of applications was rejected in 1974, he quit work and moved to North Carolina with his girlfriend, Elizabeth. After living a semi-retired life of leisure for three months, he then resumed working as a lab technician.

Cohen also left the big city in 1974, accepting a position as an arts and crafts teacher at Highland Community School, a residential facility for emotionally disturbed teens located on a 600-acre farm near Paradox, New York, in the Adirondack Mountains. He enjoyed this more self-sufficient, rustic life, and even constructed his own house.

In 1976, Greenfield also moved back to the country. In 1977, the two friends met up again. Both men agreed their careers weren't exactly satisfying and they wanted to try something different. The two thought about what they wanted to do, and they eventually decided they wanted to live in a rural college town and open a food business that they could run in a fun, creative manner.

They first considered making bagels, but discovered that the equipment needed was too expensive. Finally, they decided to try making ice cream. Both Cohen and Greenfield had had some limited experience with the treat during their lives. As a child, Cohen had often made his own ice-cream concoctions by stirring cookies and candy into his ice cream, and he had enjoyed his stints working for the neighborhood ice-cream truck. Also, while he was working at Highland School, he and his students had experimented with making homemade ice cream. Greenfield had worked as a part-time ice-cream scooper in the Oberlin cafeteria.

After a little bit of research, the two discovered that for only five dollars each they could take a correspondence course in ice-cream making from Penn State University. Both men received perfect scores on their final exam for the course, and afterwards, they began scouting for a place to open their store.

"Good Will, Good Times, Good Ice Cream"

Cohen and Greenfield would have liked to stay in New York State, but the town they wanted to settle in—Saratoga Springs—already had an ice-cream parlor and they realized the small population could not support another one. Their second choice was Burlington, Vermont, a relatively small city and the home of the University of Vermont. The two pooled $8,000 of their own money along with a $4,000 loan and refurnished an old gas station on a downtown street corner in Burlington. On May 5, 1978, Ben & Jerry's Homemade opened for business with the promise of providing "good will, good times, and good ice cream."

Greenfield refined their recipe for their first batch of ice cream, which included vanilla and 11 other flavors. The ice cream was cranked in an old-fashioned rock-salt ice-cream maker, using milk and cream from nearby dairy farms. Not all of their attempts to gain the proper consistency were successful, but their rich, homemade ice cream, unusual flavors, and rapidly improving quality quickly attracted an enthusiastic following among Burlington residents.

During the first year, Greenfield worked primarily as the ice-cream maker while Cohen worked on sales, advertising, and ingredient acquisition. Determined to keep their venture as fun and colorful as possible, Cohen dreamed up innovative ways to advertise the product while entertaining customers. His most successful scheme in the store's first summer was a free movie festival, during which feature films were projected against one of the walls of their building.

GROWING PAINS

Despite the growing popularity of their ice cream, Cohen and Greenfield recognized that in order to be successful, they could not simply rely on walk-in business to their store. Cohen convinced area restaurants to serve Ben & Jerry's premium ice cream, and then delivered the product to them in his station wagon. By 1980, their customer list included grocery stores and convenience stores. In order to meet the growing demand, Cohen and Greenfield rented an abandoned spool and bobbin factory in Burlington, which allowed them to produce ice cream in greater quantities. Rather than using a slick corporate advertising campaign, they began packing their product in pint cartons plastered with their photographs. "The image we wanted," Cohen remarked, "was grass roots."

Ben & Jerry's Homemade grew far more quickly than the two owners had ever imagined. Unschooled in business techniques, they became overwhelmed by the demands of running the expanding operations. At one point, they had to shut down the store for a day just to manage all the paperwork and pay the bills. In their usual playful manner, they posted a sign on their store that said, "We're closed because we're trying to figure out what's going on."

Production methods changed as the company grew larger. Today, Ben & Jerry's Homemade Ice Cream is mixed in 1,000 gallon stainless steel mega-blenders, then transferred to smaller vats where flavors are added. The mix is frozen (from 36° F to 22° F) and chunks or swirls are blended in. Finally, the ice cream is packaged and hardened to -10° F for shipping. The company continues to purchase its milk and cream from the St. Albans, Vermont, Cooperative Creamery and to practice quality controls to retain the homemade taste of its ice cream.

Cartons of Ben & Jerry's ice cream sold in 2004. The top four flavors that year were Cherry Garcia, Chocolate Chip Cookie Dough, Chocolate Fudge Brownie, and Chunky Monkey.

In 1981, Cohen and Greenfield moved their ice-cream plant to a much larger building that could accommodate more production. They opened a second store in Shelbourne, Vermont, but remained determined to keep their operation local. It was important to them that their business be a part of a small community, rather than expanding into an impersonal corporate empire. In 1981, however, a rare opportunity fell into their lap. A cover story in *Time* magazine described Ben & Jerry's as the "best ice cream in the world." Cohen saw a chance to turn that description into an endorsement. The magazine's words of praise firmly established their ice cream, as of yet unknown outside of Vermont, as a rare delicacy worth obtaining at great expense.

Accelerating demand for their ice cream led Cohen and Greenfield to begin franchising their stores. In 1983, Ben & Jerry's moved out of state for the first time as a franchise opened in Portland, Maine, and pints were sold in Boston-area stores through an independent distributor.

THE PROBLEMS OF BIG BUSINESS

The growth of the company from a small, owner-operated ice-cream parlor to a multimillion-dollar business would have been a dream come true for

There were 300 Ben & Jerry Scoop Shops like this one in the U.S. in 2005; another 150 located in other countries around the world.

most entrepreneurs, but it created a crisis of conscience for Greenfield and Cohen. As Cohen explained, "When Jerry and I realized we were no longer ice cream men but businessmen, our first reaction was to sell." They were afraid of what would happen if they brought in the business experts needed to deal with the complex financial matters involved in such a large business. They envisioned their fun-loving enterprise becoming a faceless corporation concerned with profits at the expense of workers and losing its close ties to the community.

Greenfield, in fact, did choose to step away from the business for awhile. In 1982, he moved to Arizona with Elizabeth as she pursued her doctorate degree in psychology. Although he kept in touch, he left Cohen to handle the bulk of the business decisions. Meanwhile, as Cohen mulled over the matter, he wondered if they might somehow be able to use the size and wealth of their business to act for the betterment of a larger community. He wanted to use the company to accomplish on a large scale what they had previously been doing on a much smaller one.

Cohen decided to accept the challenge and try to adapt his ideals to the structure of a large organization. Operating as the company's chief executive officer (CEO), he hired the business experts he needed but formulated some of his own radical guidelines under which they would operate, such as the rule that the highest-paid executives could earn no more than five times the pay of the lowest-level employee. He initiated a sale of public stock to raise more working funds for the operations—but invoked a little-known state law that allowed him to offer the company stock only to Vermont residents (this practice was later discontinued). The stock sale enabled Ben & Jerry's to construct a large new plant and company headquarters in Waterbury, Vermont.

Even as it grew, the company continued to build on its wacky, irreverent, fun-loving image. In 1983, Ben & Jerry's supplied the ice cream for the world's largest sundae—a 27,000-pound monstrosity created in St. Albans, Vermont. It also showed a more serious side. Cohen demonstrated that he meant what he said about using the corporation as a vehicle for improving social conditions. In 1984, he started a policy of donating 7.5 percent of the company's pre-tax profits to charity, and he created the Ben & Jerry's Foundation for funding community-aid projects.

THE SOCIALLY CONSCIOUS COMPANY

Cohen's passionate commitment to running a different, socially conscious kind of company appealed to Greenfield, who came back on board in 1985 as Director of Mobile Operations. One of Greenfield's primary responsibilities when he returned was facilitating an employee-led, morale-boosting program called the Joy Gang. The group enlivened the work atmosphere by doing such things as sponsoring an "Elvis Day" and encouraging Halloween costumes at work. Employees received many other benefits as well, including free gym memberships, a day-care service, help with college tuition, and three free pints of Ben & Jerry's ice cream every day.

Throughout the 1980s, the company followed a revolutionary business plan that combined zaniness with social activism. In 1986, Cohen and Greenfield took to the road in a converted mobile home known as the Cowmobile, intending to travel across the country distributing free ice cream along the way. The tour lasted four months until the Cowmobile caught fire near Cleveland and was destroyed. They made a more successful tour the following year in a mobile home dubbed Cow II. Ben & Jerry's gave ever more whimsical names to its new ice-cream flavors, such as "Cherry Garcia," named in honor of legendary rock guitarist Jerry Garcia of the Grateful Dead, and "Economic Crunch" after the stock market recession. It also won favor with the public by giving out free ice cream every year on the anniversary of its start in business.

One of the company's most famous flavors—Chunky Monkey, a blend of banana ice cream with walnuts and chocolate chunks—was suggested and named by a college student in New Hampshire.

Cohen and Greenfield often stated that Ben & Jerry's had "a social mission" in addition to an economic and a product mission. They believed a successful company could use "caring capitalism" to help build successful communities as well. For example, in 1987, the company developed a flavor called Chocolate Fudge Brownie, packed with brownies made by homeless people in Yonkers, New York. Ben & Jerry's also cosponsored the One Percent for Peace program, a nonprofit group that advocated redirecting national resources in order to support world peace.

Ben & Jerry's has had flavors commemorating such cultural icons as the Doonesbury and Dilbert cartoons, as well as the sitcom *Seinfeld* and rock band Phish.

The company showed its commitment to the environment as well. It used only all-natural ingredients and growth-hormone-free milk in its

The pigs that were fed the ice-cream waste products ate all flavors with equal enthusiasm—except for Mint-Oreo Cookie.

products. It also reduced environmental impact by feeding waste from ice-cream production to pigs on a farm in Stowe, Vermont, and using packaging made from recycled materials. Many of Ben & Jerry's products directly supported environmental causes as well. For example, RainForest Crunch was made with nuts harvested by native people in the Amazon rain forest. The ice cream helped create an incentive to grow the trees and nuts rather than destroying the habitat for farmland. Also, 60 percent of the flavor's profits were donated to rain forest preservation efforts.

CONTINUED GROWTH

Traditional business experts often cringed at what they viewed as Ben & Jerry's antibusiness approach to business. Critics were skeptical of the company's folksy, good-guy image, calling its founders self-righteous and self-promoting. Nonetheless, Ben & Jerry's rich, flavorful ice cream (its butterfat content can range as high as 17 percent, much higher than most ice creams) and offbeat style fueled remarkable growth. In 1984, the company more than doubled its sales to $4 million. Those figures grew to $9 million in 1985, $20 million the following year, and $32 million in 1987. By the close of the twentieth century, the company was grossing more than $237 million in annual sales. Because of the success of Ben & Jerry's and its contributions to the community, in 1988 Cohen and Greenfield were awarded the U.S. Small Business Persons of the Year honor by President Ronald Reagan.

Not everything the company touched turned to gold, however. In the late 1980s, Ben & Jerry's attempted to market a low-fat ice-cream product. The attempt was a disaster, largely because Ben & Jerry's primary appeal was to customers more concerned with rich taste than with calories. But in the 1990s, the company steered around the problem by finding a more appealing way to cut calories from its products: a line of frozen yogurt. At about the same time, it wrestled with the problem of including cookie dough into an ice cream, a pet dream of the owners. For years they could not find a way to keep the dough from clogging the equipment. But after five years of research, the problem was solved, and the resulting product became Ben & Jerry's most popular flavor.

The delicious result of mixing chunks of cookie dough into ice cream was introduced to the world in 1991 and remained one of the top favorite Ben and Jerry's flavors 14 years later.

Despite its success, however, Ben & Jerry's continued to experience conflict and tension because of the ideals of its owners, the demands of a growing business, and the attitudes of those trained in more traditional business practices. Beginning in 1986, the company could no longer meet production demands on its own, and needed to begin contracting out some of its ice-cream production to other plants. Two years later, Ben & Jerry's expanded its market into Canada. Because of these and other changes, Cohen and Greenfield found themselves having to compromise on such issues as pay scale and the need for increasing automation at the plant, all while trying to protect their employees' jobs and benefits.

When sales tapered off and the company suffered its first quarterly loss ever in 1994, Cohen decided he had taken the business as far as he could. In looking for a replacement to head the company, however, he took the typical Ben & Jerry's offbeat approach. He set up the "Yo! I'm Your CEO!" contest and asked prospective executives to submit essays describing why they were the right person to run the company. The contest drew more than 20,000 entries. (In the end, however, the new CEO was actually chosen by a professional search firm.)

Cohen and Greenfield remained active in running the business until April 2000, when they sold the company to Unilever, a European corporation, for $326 million. They approved the sale only after gaining assurances that the company would continue the socially responsible policies for which Ben &

Jerry's was known. Following the sale, Cohen and Greenfield continued their involvement with humanitarian and social issues.

LEGACY

Ben Cohen and Jerry Greenfield grew their corner ice-cream parlor into a nationally recognized company. They did so largely by accident, as their distinctive and creative approach to business earned their products recognition beyond their expectations. By becoming known as the fun little company that swam against the current of the corporate world, Ben & Jerry's achieved something close to hero status. By 2003, the company's products could be purchased in countries around the world, including Israel, South Korea, the United Kingdom, and Belgium. Its popularity climbed so high that the Waterbury ice cream plant became Vermont's most visited tourist attraction.

Many business experts give Cohen and Greenfield credit for changing the way large businesses view their role in society. Cohen and Greenfield were key figures in the founding of Business for Social Responsibility, an association whose members believe businesses can be profitable while still promoting social equality and environmental consciousness. Other members of the organization include Adidas, The Body Shop USA, and the Ford Motor Company.

The impact of Ben & Jerry's revolutionary and sometimes controversial business philosophy has yet to be determined. But the company's effort to

Ben Cohen (left) and Jerry Greenfield told students at DePauw University, Greencastle, Indiana, that they have the ability and the responsibility to make the world a better place. The entrepreneurs discussed their non-traditional business practices in November 2002.

de-emphasize profits, while focusing on community relations and improving the quality of life for its workers and for society in general, struck a chord with many people. In a time when many individuals feel helpless against the economic power wielded by giant, faceless corporations, it can be comforting to know some companies are still operating with a mom-and-pop attitude. While Greenfield's stated business maxim of "If it isn't fun, why do it?" may not represent the traditional approach to business, it reflects an attitude that most workers welcome in their employers.

The Ice Cream Gourmet

Although ice cream was a popular dessert as far back as the eighteenth century, the concept of a "super-premium" ice cream like that of Ben & Jerry's, is relatively new.

The idea of a gourmet ice cream may have originated with Rubin Mattus. During the early 1920s, Mattus drove a horse-drawn cart around the streets of the Bronx in New York, selling ice cream and other frozen dessert products for his family's business. Mattus became engrossed in the world of cool confections and dreamed of creating the finest ice-cream products ever known. Over many years, he built up business experience, until in 1961 he was ready to make his dream come true.

Mattus created a new ice-cream company that he called Häagen-Dazs—a name he hoped would project an image of Old-World European tradition and craftsmanship. Using the finest, most costly ingredients he could find, he began selling three flavors of his super-premium ice cream: vanilla, strawberry, and chocolate. Mattus then began traveling around the world, driven by the desire to find the most delicious ingredients and new flavors. Other companies may have produced affordable ice cream, but Mattus decided to appeal solely to consumers' taste buds instead.

At first, Mattus had a hard time finding stores to carry his products because many distributors were afraid that no one would be willing to pay the extremely high prices set for premium ice cream. But Mattus was persistent, and he knew that eventually people would be won over by his ice cream's high quality. Starting out on a small scale, Häagen-Dazs was originally sold only in New York ice-cream shops. Mattus's instincts proved correct—rave reviews from customers created a strong demand for his products. The business expanded rapidly, and by 1973 Häagen-Dazs was sold in most areas of the United States.

By the early 1980s, competitors had entered into the premium ice cream market, one of which was Ben & Jerry's. Häagen-Dazs (which was purchased by Pillsbury in 1983) waged a fierce competition against Ben & Jerry's when the young company began encroaching on its market. The battle eventually ended up in the courts. Pillsbury threatened to stop selling Häagen-Dazs to retailers who also carried Ben & Jerry's; Ben & Jerry's retaliated by filing a suit against Pillsbury. Not one to do things entirely by the book, Jerry Greenfield picketed the Pillsbury corporate offices carrying a sign reading "What's the Doughboy Afraid of?" Fortunately, the matter was settled out of court, and eventually both products could be found side by side in supermarket freezers.

In 2005, Häagen-Dazs remained one of the leading names in super-premium ice cream. In addition to being sold in supermarkets, the ice cream was served in more than 700 cafes in 54 countries around the world.

GLOSSARY

bankrupt: unable to pay back one's debts. After a person or corporation is declared legally bankrupt, a court divides up the debtor's property among the creditors.

chicle: the thickened sap from a sapodilla tree, an evergreen that grows in Mexico and Central America

confection: a sweet prepared food, such as candy. People who make or sell confections are called **confectioners**.

contract: a legally binding, written agreement between two or more people

contractor: someone who agrees to provide services and/or material for a certain price. When a corporation **contracts out**, it hires a person or company outside the organization to provide services.

corn starch: the carbohydrate found in corn kernels. Ground into a white powder, it is used in industry and as a thickener in cooking.

corn syrup: a syrup prepared from corn starch

corporation: a business that is a legal entity, chartered by a state or the federal government, and separate and distinct from the persons who own it

cream of tartar: a white acidic powder used in baking

depression: a period of drastic decline in business production and of high unemployment

direct marketing: a sales offer delivered individually to prospective buyers

extrude: to push out through a die or mold

fiscal year: any continuous 12-month period used by a business. A fiscal year isn't always the same as a calendar year.

franchise: a licensing arrangement in which an investor pays money to the owner of a particular brand-name product or business for permission to sell that product or operate that business in a certain territory. The person offering the permission is called the **franchiser**. The person buying the rights is the **franchisee**.

going public: offering shares of stock of a privately owned company to the public for the first time. The more proper term is **initial public offering (IPO)**.

grass roots: people at the local level rather than the center of politics; the source of something

hopper: a container, typically funnel shaped, in which materials are stored until needed

in-house: used to describe work performed within an organization instead of by an outside contractor

invest: to commit money to some enterprise, usually a business, in order to earn more money or some other return in the future

malted milk: a powder made of dried milk, malted barley (a grain that has been allowed to sprout), and wheat flour, often mixed with liquid milk, ice cream, and flavorings to create a thick, creamy drink

mass production: the manufacture of goods in large quantities

NASDAQ: National Association of Securities Dealers Automated Quotations, a computerized system that provides stock brokers and dealers with price quotations for securities traded

nougat: a confection made from a sugar or honey paste into which nuts are mixed

penny candy: individually wrapped small pieces of candy sold for a penny a piece

philanthropist: a person who promotes human welfare usually through giving large gifts of money

premium: something offered free or at a reduced price as an enticement to buy something else

profit margin: the amount of money a company charges for a product above its cost to make and sell that product

public ownership: a company whose shares are owned by the general public and traded (bought and sold) on a stock exchange

real estate: land and whatever is on it, including any natural resources and developments

recession: a period of general decline in business activity

refinery: an industrial plant for purifying a substance such as sugar or oil

revenue: income from an investment, business, or property

shareholder: someone who owns a portion of a company, in the form of shares of stock

stock: shares of ownership of a corporation

stock exchange: an organized marketplace where stocks of companies are bought and sold

sucrose: one of many different types of sugar

sugar cane: a tall tropical southeast Asian grass with thick, solid stems that are a source of sugar

trust: a financial relationship in which a person or company holds the title to property or money for the benefit of another person or company. A **trust fund** is the property or money.

wholesale: the sale of goods in large quantities, usually for resale by a retailer. The retailer increases the price of items sold individually.

BIBLIOGRAPHY

Amos, Wally. "A Letter to Readers from Wally Amos, Founder of Famous Amos Cookies." http://ye.entreworld.org/1-2000/mentmess.cfm.

Amos, Wally, with Camilla Denton. *Man with No Name: Turn Lemons into Lemonade.* Lower Lake, Calif.: Aslan Publishing, 1994.

Amos, Wally, and Stu Glauberman. *Watermelon Magic: Seeds of Wisdom, Slices of Life.* Hillsboro, Ore.: Words Publishing, 1996.

Amos, Wally, with Eden Lee Murray. *The Cookie Never Crumbles: Inspirational Recipes for Everyday Living.* New York: St. Martin's Press, 2001.

Amos, Wally, and Leroy Robinson. *The Famous Amos Story: The Face That Launched a Thousand Chips.* New York: Doubleday, 1983.

Arai, Juliette. "History." Krispy Kreme Doughnut Corporation Records, ca. 1937-1997 #594. Smithsonian National Museum of American History: Behring Center. http://americanhistory.si.edu/archives/d9594.htm.

Armour, Stephanie. "Executive Suites Come at a Price." USA Today, February 17, 1999.

"Ben Cohen and Jerry Greenfield." *Current Biography Yearbook 1994*, April. New York: H. W. Wilson, 1994.

Ben & Jerry's. "Our Company." http://www.benjerry.com/our_company/.

Biography on A&E. "Amos, Wally." http://search.biography.com/print_record.pl?id=23645.

Book, Esther Wachs. *Why the Best Man for the Job Is a Woman: The Unique Female Qualities of Leadership.* New York: HarperBusiness, 2000.

Brenner, Jöel Glenn. *The Emperors of Chocolate: Inside the Secret World of Hershey and Mars.* New York: Random House, 1999.

Burford, Betty. *Chocolate by Hershey: A Story about Milton S. Hershey.* Minneapolis: Carolrhoda Books, 1994.

Burke, Ray. "The Bee, the Reed, the Root: The History of Sugar." http://www2.gasou.edu/gsufl/sugar/sugar-b.htm.

Candy USA. "All about Candy." http://www.CandyUSA.org/AllAboutCandy/AAC_index.shtml.

———. "Statistical Information." http://www.CandyUSA.org/Stats/statsindex.shtml.

The Chewing Gum World. "Wrigley Success Story over the World." http://www.members.lycos.fr/chewinggumworld/wrigleyh.htm.

Cleary, David Powers. *Great American Brands: The Success Formulas That Made Them Famous.* New York: Fairchild Publications, 1981.

Cohen, Sherry Suib. "Beyond Macho." *Working Woman*, February 1989.

Fishman, Charles. "The King of Kreme." http://www.fastcompany.com/magazine/28/krispy.html.

Fucini, Joseph J., and Suzy Fucini. *Entrepreneurs: The Men and Women behind Famous Brand Names and How They Made It.* Boston: G. K. Hall, 1985.

Hershey Foods Corporation. http://www.hersheys.com/index_html.asp.

Hostess. "Media Room." http://www.twinkies.com.

International Directory of Company Histories. 55 vols. Chicago: St. James Press, 1988-.

Jampolsky, Gerald G. *One Person Can Make a Difference: Ordinary People Doing Extraordinary Things.* New York: Bantam Books, 1990.

Krispy Kreme. "Online Press Kit." http://www.krispykreme.com/mediarelations.html.

Mars, Incorporated. "About M&Ms." http://www.mms.com/us/about/.

———. "About Us." http://www.mars.com/About_us/.

Milton Hershey School. "Story Behind the School." http://www.mhs-pa.org/default.asp?id=371.

Nestlé. "History of Nestlé Toll House." http://www.VeryBestBaking.com/products/tollhouse/history.asp.

Pottker, Jan. *Crisis in Candyland: Melting the Shell of the Mars Family Empire.* Bethesda, Md.: National Press Books, 1995.

Serwer, Andy. "The Hole Story." *Fortune*, July 7, 2003.

Sterling Speakers. "Wally Amos: Turning Lemons into Lemonade." http://www.sterlingspeakers.com/amos.htm.

Sugar Knowledge International. "How Sugar Is Made." http://www.sucrose.com/lhist.html.

Tootsie Roll Industries, Inc. "Company History." http://www.tootsie.com/history.html.

Trillin, Calvin. *American Stories.* New York: Ticknor and Fields, 1991.

Wardlaw, Lee. *Bubblemania: The Chewy History of Bubble Gum.* New York: Aladdin Paperbacks, 1997.

Wilkinson, Stephen. "The Practical Genius of Penny Candy." *Working Woman*, April 1989.

Wm. Wrigley Jr. Company. http://www.wrigley.com/wrigley/index.asp.

SOURCE NOTES

Introduction

p. 8 : Ray Burke, "The Bee, the Reed, the Root: The History of Sugar," http://www2.gasou.edu/gsufl/sugar/sugar-b.htm.

Chapter One

pp. 17-18: David Powers Cleary, *Great American Brands: The Success Formulas That Made Them Famous* (New York: Fairchild Publications, 1981), 166.

p. 21: Cleary, *Great American Brands*, 167.

p. 23: Jöel Glenn Brenner, *The Emperors of Chocolate: Inside the Secret World of Hershey and Mars* (New York: Random House, 1999), 83.

p. 25: Brenner, *Emperors of Chocolate*, 154.

p. 27 (margin): Brenner, *Emperors of Chocolate*, 90.

p. 27: Brenner, *Emperors of Chocolate*, 89.

p. 30: Brenner, *Emperors of Chocolate*, 109.

p. 31: Cleary, *Great American Brands*, 169.

p. 32 (margin): Brenner, *Emperors of Chocolate*, 115.

p. 32: Brenner, *Emperors of Chocolate*, 131.

p. 38: Brenner, *Emperors of Chocolate*, 117.

p. 39: Milton Hershey School, "Story Behind the School," http://www.mhs-pa.org/default.asp?id=371.

Chapter Two

p. 42: Cleary, *Great American Brands*, 288.

p. 43: Joseph J. Fucini and Suzy Fucini, *Entrepreneurs: The Men and Women behind Famous Brand Names and How They Made It* (Boston: G. K. Hall, 1985), 25.

p. 45: Cleary, *Great American Brands*, 288.

p. 49 (first and second): Cleary, *Great American Brands*, 289.

p. 53: Cleary, *Great American Brands*, 289.

Chapter Three

p. 60: Brenner, *Emperors of Chocolate*, 52.

p. 61: Brenner, *Emperors of Chocolate*, 53.

p. 65: Brenner, *Emperors of Chocolate*, 60.

p. 66: Brenner, *Emperors of Chocolate*, 66.

p. 69 (caption): Brenner, *Emperors of Chocolate*, 157.

p. 70: Brenner, *Emperors of Chocolate*, 186.

Chapter Four

pp. 75-76: Andy Serwer, "The Hole Story," *Fortune*, July 7, 2003, 53.

p. 78: Juliette Arai, "History," Krispy Kreme Doughnut Corporation Records, ca. 1937-1997 #594 (Smithsonian National Museum of American History: Behring Center), http://americanhistory.si.edu/archives/d9594.htm.

p. 80: Hostess, "Media Room," http://www.twinkies.com.

p. 85: Serwer, "The Hole Story," 52.

Chapter Five

p. 96: Stephen Wilkinson, "The Practical Genius of Penny Candy," *Working Woman*, April 1989, 104.

p. 99: Wilkinson, "The Practical Genius of Penny Candy," 102.

p. 102 (margin): Wilkinson, "The Practical Genius of Penny Candy," 102.

p. 102 (first): Sherry Suib Cohen, "Beyond Macho," *Working Woman*, February 1989, 79.

p. 102 (second): Wilkinson, "The Practical Genius of Penny Candy," 104.

pp. 103-104: Stephanie Armour, "Executive Suites Come at a Price," *USA Today*, February 17, 1999.

p. 106: Wilkinson, "The Practical Genius of Penny Candy," 102.

p. 107 (first): Esther Wachs Book, *Why the Best Man for the Job Is a Woman: The Unique Female Qualities of Leadership* (New York: HarperBusiness, 2000), 171.

p. 107 (second): Book, *Why the Best Man for the Job Is a Woman*, 187.

p. 108 (first and second): Wilkinson, "The Practical Genius of Penny Candy," 104.

p. 109 (caption): Wilkinson, "The Practical Genius of Penny Candy," 104.

p. 109: Book, *Why the Best Man for the Job Is a Woman*, 174.

Chapter Six

p. 112 (margin): Wally Amos with Eden Lee Murray, *The Cookie Never Crumbles: Inspirational Recipes for Everyday Living* (New York: St. Martin's Press, 2001), 22.

p. 115 (margin): Amos, *The Cookie Never Crumbles*, 35.

p. 116: Wally Amos and Leroy Robinson, *The Famous Amos Story: The Face That Launched a Thousand Chips* (New York: Doubleday, 1983), 31.

p. 117: Sterling Speakers, "Wally Amos: Turning Lemons into Lemonade," http://www.sterlingspeakers.com/amos.htm.

p. 119: Sterling Speakers, "Wally Amos: Turning Lemons into Lemonade."

p. 120 (margin): Wally Amos and Stu Glauberman, *Watermelon Magic: Seeds of Wisdom, Slices of Life* (Hillsboro, Ore.: Words Publishing, 1996), 65.

p. 121 (caption): Amos, *Watermelon Magic*, 33.

p. 124 (margin): Amos , *Watermelon Magic*, 25.

p. 124: Sterling Speakers, "Wally Amos: Turning Lemons into Lemonade."

Chapter Seven

p. 129: "Ben Cohen and Jerry Greenfield," *Current Biography Yearbook 1994*, April (New York: H. W. Wilson, 1994), 121.

p. 130: "Ben Cohen and Jerry Greenfield," *Current Biography Yearbook 1994*, 121.

p. 133: Ben & Jerry's, "Our Company," http://www.benjerry.com/our_company/.

p. 134 (first and second): "Ben Cohen and Jerry Greenfield," *Current Biography Yearbook 1994*, 122.

p. 135: "Ben Cohen and Jerry Greenfield," *Current Biography Yearbook 1994*, 122.

p. 137: "Ben Cohen and Jerry Greenfield," *Current Biography Yearbook 1994*, 122.

p. 139 (first and second): "Ben Cohen and Jerry Greenfield," *Current Biography Yearbook 1994*, 123.

p. 142: "Ben Cohen and Jerry Greenfield," *Current Biography Yearbook 1994*, 123.

p. 144: "Ben Cohen and Jerry Greenfield," *Current Biography Yearbook 1994*, 120.

p. 145 (essay): Calvin Trillin, *American Stories* (New York: Ticknor and Fields, 1991), 151-152.

INDEX

ABOUT THE AUTHOR

Nathan Aaseng is an award-winning author of more than 100 fiction and nonfiction books for young readers. He writes on subjects ranging from science and technology to business, government, politics, and law. Aaseng's books for The Oliver Press include seven titles in the **Business Builders** series and nine titles in the **Great Decisions** series. He lives with his wife, Linda, and their four children in Eau Claire, Wisconsin.

PHOTO CREDITS